SUSAN SLY & SUZAN HART

MLM Woman

20 READY TO USE TIPS FROM PROFESSIONAL
NETWORKERS TO DEVELOP AND GROW YOUR
NETWORK MARKETING BUSINESS

1st Printing, January 2008

Printed in United States of America

ISBN 13: 978-193305764-4

We lovingly dedicate this book to women everywhere who truly believe they can be more and build the life of their dreams as an entrepreneur.

Susan & Suzan

Many Thanks

We gratefully acknowledge all of the women who contributed their stories and were willing to share their journey.

Thank you to Sound Concepts, Mac and JJ, for believing in the project.

Lastly, thank you to all of the wonderful women mentors who have touched our lives and believed in us. Thank you to Kathy Coover, Kathy Smith, Carole Taylor, Renata Lee, Deborah Kay and Erica Combs.

"Don't limit yourself. Many people limit themselves to what they think they can do. You can go as far as your mind lets you. What you believe, remember, you can achieve." -Mary Kay Ash

Table of Contents

What Is MLM?

MLM stands for multilevel marketing. Did you know that every woman is an entrepreneur at heart? Within each and every one of us lies brilliance and magnificence. We are all able to get the job done when it comes to building and growing a massive home based business. Every woman is a natural networker.

Have you ever referred a friend to a movie, a television show or a book? Have you ever spoken passionately about a favorite restaurant, vacation, hair salon or massage therapist? Have you ever had to 'enroll' your children into getting ready for school on time or doing their homework? If you answered 'yes' to any of these questions then you have already entered the world of selling. You are a multilevel marketer.

As women we are indeed very passionate when it comes to sharing our likes, dislikes and feelings. When we love something we tell a few people. When we are upset or dislike something, we tell several people. In fact, as women we tend to live longer because we express our emotions. According to Dr. John Gray, author of *Men are from Mars, Women are from Venus*, women actually boost their serotonin or 'happy chemical' when they talk to other women. It is no wonder that 82% of the network marketing industry in America is women driven.

Network, multilevel marketing or referral based marketing is as old as time. In ancient days whether you were selling clay pots or silks your customers came from word of mouth marketing. In the early twentieth century companies caught on to this notion that people should be paid to refer others to products. Industry leaders like Amway and Mary Kay

Cosmetics paved the way for the network marketing companies we know today.

Thanks to super computers, cost effective calling plans and the ever evolving home office it is now possible for women to make a significant income in network marketing from the comfort of their own home. In fact this is the best time to get started. No matter what is happening in the economy women will continue to do what we have done for millennia – we will refer our friends, neighbors and families to the things we love.

Network marketing has evolved so much that celebrities and authors such as Donald Trump, Robert Kiosaki of *Rich Dad Poor Dad* fame, T. Harv Eker, author of *Secrets of the Millionaire Mind*, Warren Buffet, billionaire and many others endorse network marketing as a legitimate business. When we look to the future of the industry it has never been more clear. We are part of a global movement to provide effective products at a reasonable price using internet marketing. Be prepared, this is a wave that is growing in momentum.

Let's think about this for a moment. How many of you have ever purchased something online? From Amazon to the Home Shopping Channel, people are becoming more accustomed to picking up the phone or logging in. This technology is picking up momentum at a feverish pitch. Just think about Black Friday, the day in America that logs the biggest sales prior to the holiday season. Imagine fighting the crowds, trying to find parking, waiting in line while you sweat beneath your coat, dealing with unhappy people and coming to the brink of near starvation as you try and find that perfect gift. Do you feel ill? Of course, very few people wish to deal with that.

Now think about getting up in your pajamas with a steaming mug of your favorite warm drink, logging onto the computer in the relative tranquility of your home and shopping online. A few days later your goods arrive. There was no parking hassle, no lines and no distractions. It was faster and more efficient. Internet shopping is here to stay and that is why everyone from small boutiques to large retailers like the Gap and Neiman Marcus allow you to shop in their virtual stores.

Network marketing is the exact same way. It is word of mouth marketing without the cost of expensive television, radio or print advertising. When you purchase an expensive pair of sneakers the manufacturer's cost is very low compared to the millions they paid the celebrity or athlete to endorse the products. In direct sales or network marketing, the endorsement fee is paid to the individual who does the referrals. The best part is that you didn't have to win an Olympic gold medal, Wimbledon or the L.P.G.A. tour to get paid your fee. It is democracy in its finest form.

HOW TO EVALUATE A COMPANY

MLM is one of the finest forms of business in the world. This is truly an industry where the average person can create an extraordinary income. The tax write offs alone warrant a serious look. In addition to the successes we hear horror stories of people getting 'ripped off' in network marketing. The simple truth is that often these people did not research the company because they either did not take the time or were not equipped with the evaluation skills.

Network marketing is actually very simple. A company will create a product or service. They will hopefully test it on a group of people before releasing it. Company officials usually give their friends, family and business associates prime positioning by 'sponsoring' them first. From there the sales force grows by word of mouth or referral marketing. Ideally, a company has adequate start-up capital and infrastructure to maintain growth.

Dr. Charles King identified some very basic phases of growth in network marketing companies. These phases are useful in identifying where a company is at in terms of viability. Thousands of companies are created, however very few actually make an impact and create millionaires. The successful ones follow the stages of growth. The stages are: formulation, concentration, critical mass, momentum and stability. Each stage is highly important. Network marketing is a serious business and if you are to create a serious income then a fundamental understanding of your industry is paramount.

Formulation is the initial phase. In this stage a product or service is being created. It is run through trials and often reformulated again. If it is a consumable product, factors such as taste, packaging, shipping, texture, expiration, cost of raw materials, testing and product stability are factored in. Creating a nutrition product is very expensive by the time one looks at safety of ingredients, sourcing the materials, manufacturing and trials. Good products stay in formulation until the company gets it right.

The next 'litmus' test is called concentration, where the products are being marketed to more and more people and growth is happening exponentially. The company may then go on to critical mass. This is the stage where most companies either sink or swim. In fact many companies actually die in this period. In critical mass, infrastructure is truly tested. Does the company have enough money to handle growth? Can they staff, manufacture and develop more products? Are they well capitalized?

Once a company passes critical mass they go into momentum. This is where the majority of new distributors come in. In momentum a company sees great growth. Infrastructure is also tested here as there may be a need for faster, higher powered computer systems, new websites, more staff, greater production demands, more capitalization and legal fees. The bigger and faster a company grows, the greater the needs. As a cautionary note, if the owners of a company are not prepared for growth and have large egos they may not survive momentum as they must be humble enough to admit when they need help.

The last stage is stability. In stability the sales are consistent. This happens with older companies. It is not that the opportunity has died, it is that companies gain brand recognition, which may or may not be good, and it becomes more difficult for distributors to achieve greater incomes.

Understanding these five phases is essential in evaluating a successful MLM opportunity. Evaluation of a company also requires a practical approach. If you were starting your own company would you interview people or would you hire just anyone? Naturally you would interview people. The same is true with your network marketing company.

You want to do your research before you make a decision. Network marketing is such a rewarding industry, however, you can avoid trial and error with companies if you know how to spot a good one.

In addition to the stages of growth identified by Dr. King it is imperative to look for other markers in any network marketing company. We have identified seven key items to look for when evaluating a company. Absolutely research any MLM opportunity you are considering as it is not just their name on the brand, it is your name in partnership.

7 KEY ITEMS TO LOOK FOR IN MLM EVALUATION FOR WOMEN

1. **The company is well capitalized.** Any company must be well funded. Companies require research and development, staffing, infrastructure, computer systems, consulting, legal services, product creation and much, much more. If a company starts up and has lack of capital, it will be the distributors who bear the brunt of the insufficient funds.

2. **The compensation plan is fair.** Does the company have a compensation plan where many people are making money? Can someone come in and make more money than their sponsor? Does the compensation plan reward you for helping your team or is it self serving? These are a few of the questions to ask when looking at a compensation plan. Additionally, many compensation plans have moved to a weekly pay out as opposed to monthly.

3. **There is an actual product.** It is illegal to run a network marketing company without an actual product. There must be a physical transaction of either a consumable, usable or service based product. Ask yourself – what product is changing hands?

4. **The management team or founders have field experience in network marketing.** Would you go to a restaurant where the chef had never made a meal? Would you go to a doctor who had never practiced medicine? Of course you wouldn't. If someone is making decisions that will affect your income and business dealings you want them to be experienced.

5. **The management team or founders have at least one woman.** This is absolutely critical. This industry is 82% women and women tend to be more aware of the needs of other women.

6. **The company provides training and support.** Let's face it. Things happen and people leave companies. A company must have training systems, preferably online, and provide events, calls and other systems to train people. This way everyone has an equal opportunity to learn.

7. **The company does not make claims.** No company can claim their products cure cancer, arthritis, fibromyalgia or anything else. If a company or their distributors make medical claims it can be shut down. Likewise if distributors show their pay checks they can also be liable. When evaluating a company, make sure they do not make any false claims. Small companies will often make claims to lure distributors. As they grow the claims cease. This is just bad (and dishonest) business practice.

WHY NETWORK MARKETING FOR WOMEN?

As mentioned before, network marketing is truly a great democratic entity when you find the right vehicle. Distributors or associates are rewarded for their efforts. The greater the effort, the greater the reward if the company is a good one. By the same token, women have an excellent opportunity to create an income from home. This allows us to spend more time with our children and loved ones. It is truly a blessing when you are the right person in the right company at the right time.

Women have and will continue to be natural agents of referrals. Getting paid on those referrals is often where the challenge comes. To be candid, many women are great givers and poor receivers. They feel awkward when it comes to receiving any kind of remuneration on a personal level unless it is for a job.

This is why we chose to create this little MLM Woman handbook. Network marketing can free families and liberate women and men all over the world if you know how to do this business. There are many books written on the subject of network marketing however not all come from people who have actually made money. Additionally, very few are written for women who make up the heart of this industry.

We feel a social obligation to create an easy-to-read, shortened form of our years of experience in direct sales and MLM. There is so much we want to convey. However, we've kept it short and to-the-point so even women who are new to our industry can learn the tips fairly quickly. By utilizing the simple tips and reading the inspiring stories of the MLM women it is our hope that you will create your own legacy. When you come to understand that network marketing is the key to building a long lasting life of fulfillment, you will know what we have known for years – this is the best decision of our lives.

We encourage you to read this book and do the exercises. There are twenty tips in total. Each one holds importance. Do not skip any of the steps. We know that within you lies a woman of greatness. You can have it all and live the life of your dreams. The first and hardest step is getting started. We encourage you to embrace the journey and go for your goals with passion and enthusiasm.

Susan & Suzan

SUSAN'S MLM STORY

In the late nineties I was training for a triathlon and duathlon. Both sports involve being the fastest you can be in running and cycling. In triathlon there is a swim component. In duathlon, you run, bike and then do a final run. To be the best requires training, persistence, coaching, dedication, a competitive spirit, proper nutrition and rest. My goal was to be the best.

In an effort to improve my fitness I hired a coach. He was an NCAA champion and world renowned athlete. Under his coaching my times improved and it was through him that I was first introduced to network marketing. When I asked him what I could do nutritionally to get faster he suggested a product line. On the products I got leaner and felt great. He then suggested I purchase at wholesale and my journey began.

A few weeks later I invested in a $1400 box of supplements. My coach told me that I could use what I wanted and sell the rest. Unknowingly to me, I was in a network marketing company. My sponsor did not share the compensation plan, the opportunity or anything else. He did not share the bigger picture.

A year later I found myself financially devastated. I lost my health, my business, my home and was over $100,000 in debt.* Would network marketing have saved me? I am not sure. One thing I do know is that when I was forced to live on my brother-in-law's sofa, an extra $500/ month would have gone a long way.

Later that year, as I was getting my life on track I went to a women's networking group. There I met a dynamic woman who became my personal training and nutrition client. She introduced me to this amazing industry the right way. She got me reading books. She exposed me to some of the best trainers in the industry. She took me to events. I saw how incredible network marketing was.

Two years later my sponsor and I were giving a home presentation and I met an incredible woman. She was powerful, smart and energetic. I knew that there was something about her. That woman was Suzan Hart.

Together Suzan and I have partnered in a few network marketing ventures. We have been part of companies that were closed down. We have seen companies make claims. We have witnessed companies let ego take over and react instead of respond to the marketplace. All in all, we have been in the trenches. Suzan and I have also been successful in the industry. She is a great friend and partner.

In my most recent venture, I have created a million dollar income. I have co-created twenty-five six and multiple six figure women. Together with Suzan we have developed leaders and that is the most rewarding part of the business.

My husband, Chris, along with our gorgeous children, Avery, AJ, and Sarai, live the life of our dreams. We no longer worry about money and make residual income while we sleep. We have been blessed to be able to give back and donate our money to worthy causes that better the lives of women and children all over the world. Our financial freedom was created by network marketing.

My message to all of you reading this book is that dreams really do come true in this industry. Some of the best friends you will ever meet will come through network marketing. This business also provides a great deal of personal growth. For Chris and me, this has enhanced our marriage and our family life. We are so grateful to God for giving us network marketing and providing us with a vehicle where we can truly give back.

You too can live the life of your dreams. It will take courage, discipline and faith. You will be forced to reconcile negative beliefs and low self worth in order to be great in this industry. Part of the success is the woman you become on the journey, for that woman will evolve daily. Success is not a destination that you arrive at. Just reading this book and having the courage to be on this journey tells me that you are already success minded. I encourage you to go for your dreams with passion. Everything you are seeking is there if you can commit to this amazing journey and the industry of MLM.

Susan

*You can read more about Susan's journey in her book *The Have It All Woman* available through www.soundconcepts.com, www.stepintoyourpower.com, and finer retailers.

SUZAN'S MLM STORY

The way you look at life can change slowly over time or it can change in an instant. My life changing event occurred in the spring of 2000. At that time I was managing a women's shelter just north of the city of Toronto. I remember walking into my office to find all my belongings packed up in a box on my desk. Before I had an opportunity to ask any questions, I found myself being escorted to the executive director's office. What was to happen next challenged every belief that had ever guided me. I walked into the executive director's office and was informed that I was being let go. Yes, I was being fired with no warning. I was devastated. I thought of all the long hours I had worked, how I had contributed to the growth of the organization. I thought of the recent promotion and glowing evaluations I had received. I remember driving home with tears streaming down my face. I was hurt, scared and unsure what to do. However on that drive home I made the decision that would change my destiny. I vowed that never again would I leave my financial security in the hands of someone else.

Although I regained employment, how I viewed my world began to change. I realized that I had contributed to organization both large and small but had little to show for it. I had risen through the ranks and was well recognized in my field and still found myself overworked and not being paid what I believed I deserved. The reality was I was $50,000 in credit card debt and borrowing from Peter to pay Paul. My marriage was falling apart. I was tired, run down and I was suffering in silence. I knew there had to be more, but more importantly, for the first time I actually believed I deserved more.

They say when the student is ready the teacher appears. Well, I was ready.

I remember sitting out in the courtyard of my townhouse complex when my neighbor Gloria walked by. She was offering all the neighbors a sample of a liquid nutrition and inviting each of us to attend a presentation at her home. As she approached me I remember saying to myself, "I'll go to be polite but I am not buying or joining anything." What I didn't know was that I was about to find the answer to my prayers.

At the meeting I sat through a very informative presentation but it was one sentence that got my attention. "I came out of retirement to introduce this product." As I looked at the presenter, Deborah, I wondered how she could be retired; she looked only a few years older than I was. From that moment, I wanted to know everything. I wanted the life she appeared to be living. After the presentation I found myself lingering, wanting to know more and in my quest for answers I connected with the second presenter. In that moment, a blessed friendship and business relationship was born.

The second presenter was Susan Sly and we connected instantly. Susan was brilliant, creative and ambitious. Like me she wanted more and I knew she had the power, drive and dedication to achieve more.

Since that day, Susan and I have journeyed together in a number of companies. We have survived companies that were closed down. We have seen companies be mismanaged, make false claims as well as over promise and under deliver. We have both put our heart into ventures and gleamed little return. But we never looked back. You see, as we learned about this amazing industry called network marketing, we knew nothing else would give us the lifestyle and freedom we were seeking.

In the last four years I have created a multiple six figure income. Susan and I have co-created leaders, dynamic women who are producing results and making their mark in this industry. We are all learning and growing along our journey and the sweetest thing is, it is just beginning.

Today I am living my dreams. I am forever grateful for that one event that shook my world and forced me to evaluate my beliefs. I firmly believe God does not give us more than we can handle. He gives us exactly what we need to make us stronger.

My thought for all who read this book is that anything you desire is possible. Network marketing is unlike any other industry. It will not only provide a vehicle for financial wealth but it will create an environment where you are able to become the best person you could ever be. Give yourself the gift of this journey. Be bold and commit to your financial, spiritual and emotional growth. Be an inspiration, for when you are bold, you inspire other women around you to believe in what's possible.

Creating abundance & ease,

Suzan

Setting Your Inspiration

BY SUZAN

"The future belongs to those who believe in the beauty of their dreams."

Eleanor Roosevelt

Have you ever asked yourself, "What is that one thing that would inspire me to act in spite of fear, challenge or potential barriers?" I have seen many educated and talented women come into network marketing and have little or no success. I have also seen women with very limited time, experience and skills arrive and achieve massive success. So what separates the two groups? It is my belief that those women who achieve success have an inspiration that fuels their actions and creates such a desire within them that failure is not an option.

A "WHY" WORTHY OF YOUR LIFE:

When I ask the questions, "What is your why?" and "What will have you achieve success?" I frequently hear "I want to buy a new car, make some extra cash or pay off debt." While these are great goals, they aren't massive enough to buy the "why worthy of your life." They aren't big enough to keep you in the game when challenge and desperation come knocking. Your why actually sits deep inside you. It is often the dream you silently have but are afraid to believe in. It is the wish you had when you were young and thought the world was your oyster. For most women their why is the deep desire they unfortunately buried as a result of surviving the ups and downs of life. When I became involved in network marketing my deepest desire was to resign from my high stress job and create a business doing what I love: training and developing others. The thought of creating income doing something I was passionate about moved me and I began to dream.

As you begin your network marketing journey, the question is, will you dare to dream? Does your company, product and services make you believe that what you desire is indeed possible? Does it cause you to begin to believe for the first time in the "why worthy of your life?" Your why is the fuel that fills your heart and makes you unstoppable. So what exactly is a massive why? Is it a goal? Or is it the result you are seeking? The why worthy of your life is often a culmination of who you become and what you achieve as well as how you are able to contribute to others along this journey.

To get in touch with your why you must be willing to let go of fear and resignation. It is to expand your thinking, to begin to transform your belief system and embrace the possibility that anything you desire is possible. It is to have such belief that you are moved to put a date to every dream you posses.

Set aside 60 minutes where you will not be disturbed. Take 5 minutes, close your eyes and imagine your network marketing business is achieving success and money is abundant. You have no concerns and all you desire is at your finger tips. How do you feel? Where are you? Who are you with? Connect with the emotions, let them wash over you. Feel and touch your surroundings. When you open your eyes, answer the following question: "If money was abundant and I had time and freedom..."

- What would I desire to do?
- What would I desire to have?
- Where would I desire to go?
- What would I desire to become?
- What would I desire to learn?
- Who would I desire to spend my time with?
- Where would I desire to live?

- How would I spend my time?
- What would be my desired legacy or contribution?
- What would be my desired passion?

ANCHORING YOUR WHY

The reality is that a "why worthy of your life" is built and reinforced by every success, big or small. In order to achieve your why it is imperative you anchor your belief in small, meaningful goals, that when achieved, make you feel closer to your life's goal.

Each 90 days, anchor your business goal to a tangible personal or family goal, a goal that, when achieved, impacts the quality of your life in such a way that you feel you have taken a small step closer to the "why worthy of your life". One of my first 90 day goals was to create enough new income for my family to take a much over due vacation. I remember how proud I felt as my family boarded the plan. I remember saying to myself, "this is just the beginning!" Every 90 days select a personal or family goal that excites you. Put a date to the goal; calculate the new money required to achieve your goal. Post your goal in a visible spot in your office.

Exercise: "The Feeling State"

In the well known movie "The Secret" they say it is not enough to think about what you want. Rather it is what you feel that creates your desire as a reality.

As you anchor your why in a personal or family goal, take time to emotionally connect to that intention. Take five minutes each day and visualize the experience of having already achieved your goals. Create a vivid story and play it for 5 minutes daily. Where are you? What are you doing? What does it feel like? Who are you with? What are you wearing?

Take five minutes and do this exercise for the next 90 days. Both Susan and I practice this daily. This small visualization is responsible for many successes.

Dealing with Desparation
BY SUSAN

"Everyone has talent. What is rare is the courage to follow the talent to the dark place where it leads."

Erica Jong, author

There comes a time in every large decision when we second guess ourselves and question our ability to achieve our goals. Having done numerous marathons I have witnessed this firsthand, finding myself with about six miles to go questioning how fast I could possibly run and making a decision to override the pain by focusing on the joy of completing the race. If you have ever given birth you also know that feeling of desperation where the pain is so intense that you question your ability to go on and then that beautiful baby comes and the pain is soon forgotten. You will encounter these moments in your network marketing career; these are the times when it seems harder to go on and much easier to quit.

Desperation shows up in your business. He knocks at your door with a bottle of Merlot or steaming hot cocoa, a warm duvet and "Sex and the City" re-runs on DVD. He says "don't make phone calls, don't bother trying to advance yourself – it is too painful. Just curl up with me in front of the television and you can try again tomorrow." Desperation is very tempting.

It is always easier to stay stuck than it is to act. Every network marketing millionaire I know, myself included, did not just walk into their success. They had to act in spite of all else. They had to do what others were not willing to do so that they could eventually live the life of their dreams.

No one wants to face rejection. None of us wants to have doors slammed, friends and family ridiculing us or people turning the other way when we walk toward them. It happens. It has happened to me. The truth is that in order to achieve greatness in your life you will have to resist desperation in all 'his' forms, including when he shows up as well meaning family members and friends who encourage you not to bother trying.

In my network marketing career I have faced desperation many times. There were occasions when I thought about going back to a regular job. The thought of having a boss really turned me off so that thought lasted only about a day. There was a time when I ran an ad in *USA Today* and one 'gentleman' left a death threat on the voicemail. That scared me for a few hours and I questioned what I was doing in network marketing and then I reasoned that there are jerks in every profession so I got back to work.

We are most vulnerable to giving up on our dreams, and ultimately ourselves, when we are tired, frustrated, ill, angry, sad and not seeing results. To be a network marketing millionaire you must stay in the game. Every millionaire and billionaire has faced these emotions. To be great you cannot quit. Outstanding athletes, business people, actors, parents, students and the like do not quit. They practice, practice, practice until they get it right and you should do the same.

You will face rejection. You will face people who tell you one thing and do another. You will encounter people who come into your business and are very excited and then disappear. You will also have people who quit. All networkers face these things and it is not unique to MLM. When I worked for a large corporation we had people quit, back stab, steal from the company, lie, cheat, not take their jobs seriously and essentially not do their job. It happens in every industry. If you haven't owned a business before or been in a management position then you simply have to be strong during these times. Suzan and I have both faced them.

If you can commit to your business, quitting will not be an option. If you can focus in and make sure you do some simple things every day to build your strength, desperation will not stand a chance. Review the following checklist to help you get through the W.K.M.s or wall kicking moments, as I call them, on the Step into Your Power C.D. series.

- Read books on personal empowerment.
- Listen to audio trainings on self mastery.
- Join a networking group.
- Educate yourself on your company's product and build your belief.
- Get at least 30 minutes of brisk exercise every day. This will keep your stress levels down and help you to be mentally sharp.
- Attend conferences and workshops.
- Create and set a schedule that works for you. (See the MLM Woman Tip on Scheduling Your Time)
- Eat healthy foods. Chemicals and food additives have been linked to mood swings.
- Drink at least 8-10 glasses of water per day. Inadequate water can increase stress.
- Get educated on the industry of network marketing.
- Subscribe to network marketing newsletters online.
- Get a good night's sleep.
- Partner with positive, like-minded people.
- See every challenge as a lesson.

My mentor taught me that the only way to fail in MLM is to quit.

Creating a Schedule That Works

BY SUZAN

*"Do today what others won't, so you can do
tomorrow what others can't."*

Unknown

Most women wear many hats: mother, wife, career woman and let's not forget taxi driver. So although many of us desire more, the thought of adding the title of entrepreneur to the list can be overwhelming, stopping us before we ever get started. When I began my network marketing career I worked 40 hours per week and traveled 2 hours each day to and from work. Like most women I ran a busy home and had all the responsibilities of a wife and mother. My only survival during those 18 months was that I created and honored a schedule.

A schedule is a clear outline of the activities you desire to achieve each day. The truth of the matter is, you cannot manage time. Time is consistent. 24 hours are in each day. However, what you can manage is how you are in time: your self mastery. When you manage the hours of your day effectively, you create a clearing for creativity, focused energy and most importantly, abundance.

A clearing is consistent space in time for a specific activity. A schedule allows you to consciously evaluate how you bring things into your day or week. It will make you prioritize tasks and activities based on importance and their ability to produce the results you desire. Here are just a few benefits of a powerful schedule:

1. **Structure:** "When and for how long." A schedule will force you to consciously evaluate how many things you can effectively manage in one day. It will help you assign a specific amount of time to each task, thus focusing your energy.

2. **Abundance:** If you look at the agenda of any successful woman, you will notice that her day is mapped out from the moment she awakes, seven days a week. Her days are abundant. She is able to achieve more in a morning than most people produce in a day. She understands that in order for the universe to deliver what she desires, she must effectively and easily manage what she has now. Both Susan and I are known for having a multitude of projects on the go at one time. I believe this is when we are at our best and the most productive. You see we have both learned how to set limits and master ourselves within time.

3. **Boundaries:** Most women come to the industry of network marketing for time freedom. Their goal is to eventually have the luxury of doing what they want, when they want, to have the privilege of participating daily in their children's lives and the choice of planning vacations when it works for their family. Although this is the intention, as lofty business goals are set, they often become the sole focus, leaving family and personal time behind. This singular focus can be devastation for family and relationships.

Abundance and balance occurs when you begin to carve out and commit specific times for various activities. When you are balanced and your day is structured, you move from the overwhelming sense of "busy" to a feeling of productivity. Now you are able to give 100% to every area of your life. This creates collaborative relationships, free of guilt because people in your life know you have created a special space for them as you produce. Setting aside personal time allows you time to replenish and nurture yourself. We cannot give to anyone when our own tank is empty.

4.   **Center Yourself:** A powerful schedule allows you to center yourself daily. It enables you to evaluate how thing are working, while taking into account the people and activities that are important to you. A schedule allows you to evaluate and course correct, therefore maintaining a clearing for abundance.

5.   **Hours of Operation:** One of the core reasons for a schedule is to ensure you have clear hours that you build your business while maintaining balance in your life. I firmly believe that if you do not have clear hours of operation, you do not truly have a business; you have a hobby. "I will do it when time permits."

As you build your schedule, map out your business hours. Share them with your family. Let your family know how they can assist you in honoring your schedule. As women we often do not ask for help. One of the biggest things I learned as I built my business was to ask, to let people in my life know how they can contribute to my success. I recommend each of you begin to develop your asking and receiving muscle.

Exercise: Building a Powerful Schedule

Commit to building an effective schedule every 90 days. Evaluate what worked in the previous 90 days and then create a new schedule based on your business, personal and family commitments. Reflect on the following questions as you build your schedule:

1. What are the inflexible demands on my time? Job, family commitments, etc.

2. What am I willing to give up to achieve what I desire?

3. When and how often will I exercise?

4. When will I have time to think, meditate and do visualizations?

5. When will I do my personal development?

6. When is my family time?

7. When do I run errands? Banking, groceries, etc.

8. When is my time for personal care?

9. When is my time for special relationships? Spouse, extended family, friends, etc.

10. When do I schedule time for fun and vacation?

11. When do I do my income producing activities?

12. When are my conference calls?

13. When do I return emails and voicemails?

13. When is my rest day?

MLM WOMAN TIP #4:

Making Your List

BY SUSAN

"You gain strength, courage and confidence by every experience in which you really stop to look fear in the face."

Eleanor Roosevelt

In over ten years of experience in network marketing I have heard more people say that they do not know anyone. To me this is truly a quitter's mentality. Any positive person would say, "I will go meet more people." Of the tens of thousands of people I have worked with I have never witnessed anyone become successful who claimed time and again that they had no 'warm market.'

A 'warm market' by definition simply refers to people you know. To extend the definition it also includes people you do not yet know. Network marketing is a relationship business. If you are under the illusion that you can simply punch email leads into an auto-responder and then go to the beach, then think again.

To make serious money in MLM you must learn how to build relationships. You want a business where people stay and not go looking for the next big thing. They will stick with you when they feel empowered by the relationship with the leader. People will remain more loyal to a leader than they will to a company. This is why your warm market offers the greatest opportunity for success. There is a network marketing adage: It is not about whom you know, it is about who they know.

Contacting people in our warm market can often be daunting. If this is how you feel then my advice to you is to build your belief. When you believe that what you have is the best and will help a great number of people, then you will not have a problem approaching potential clients in your warm market. Anyone who is afraid to speak to their friends and family does not have a big enough belief in the four areas – themselves, their product or service, their company or the industry. Sometimes they do not believe in any of these areas, in which case they have a lot of work to do.

I am known in the industry as being very direct. In other words I am not going to 'sugar coat' my advice. If you want to make it big you are going to have to talk to people. The more people you speak to about your opportunity, the more you learn. The more you learn, the more you grow. The more you grow, the more money you make so let's get to work.

I have seen car mechanics, like my friend Dave, who people would discount, become six figure earners in MLM. Many people would have discounted Dave as an overweight, middle aged guy with little desire to advance himself. Quite the opposite was true – Dave had five kids and a beautiful wife to provide for. He had big dreams.

I met one of my top leaders in a Starbucks. She was a mom of two young children looking for more in her life. You never know where you will find your leaders. Some of the best people are waiting for you and you may or may not already know them. The bottom line is never discount anyone.

There are 'diamonds' in your warm market. They may be people you come into contact with on a daily basis or they may be people you haven't seen in years. Your list is the key to your success—the larger the list the better.

I want you to imagine that you cannot fail. Everyone you speak to will be enthusiastic about what you have to offer. If you could not fail – who would you approach? Of these people, who are the most positive and open? I am going to assist you by creating some triggers. Beside each person's name, write a statement of why you want them in your business. For example:

Name	Occupation	Why They Would Be Great
Bill	Dry Cleaner	Always positive, great sense of humor

Now it's your turn – On a sheet of paper make your names list and include why each person would be great in your business.

- Child's teacher
- Dry cleaner
- Soccer coach
- Baseball coach
- Friend
- Chiropractor
- Massage therapist
- Language teacher
- Store owner
- Mortgage broker
- Hygienist
- Assistant
- Manager of local hotel
- Bank teller
- Swim instructor
- Clerk at your post office
- Car dealer
- Hair dresser
- Counter person at favorite coffee shop
- Sales person at favorite clothing store
- Physiotherapist
- Car mechanic
- Cell phone sales person

- Lawyer
- Real estate agent
- Football coach
- Neighbor
- Computer tech
- Naturopath
- Esthetician
- Tutor
- Pastor
- Investment advisor
- Nutritionist
- Receptionist
- Server at favorite restaurant
- Personal trainer
- Local athlete
- Receptionist at local health club
- Car sales person
- Architect
- Health food store owner
- Person with network marketing experience
- Grocery clerk
- Local interior decorator
- Computer sales person

- Accountant
- Dance teacher
- Hockey coach
- P.T.A. leader
- Doctor
- Acupuncturist
- Veterinarian
- Music teacher
- Client
- Dentist
- House keeper
- Banker
- Other health care professional
- Fitness instructor
- Bakery owner
- Receptionist at local spa
- Make up artist
- Engineer
- Manager of local restaurant
- Sales person at favorite jewelry store
- Delivery person
- Gym owner
- Sales person at electronics store

How did you do? How many names did you come up with? Did you find that you knew more people than you had previously thought? We all do.

Now that you have a list of contacts you are ready to start connecting. In MLM Woman Tip # 13 we will share the secrets of how to make great connections.

Designing a Mission Statement

BY SUZAN

"Emotional independence begins with the development of inner resources."

Anonymous

As you establish your new network marketing business, it is imperative that you establish a mission statement. Any successful business has a mission statement that guides it. A mission statement is a brief description of your fundamental purpose. It articulates your goals, beliefs, values and overall philosophy.

In short, it tells the world who you are, why you exist and where you are going.

A mission statement is like invisible glue, connecting you and the members of your team together. Your mission statement should be two to three sentences that create a vision that calls you to act passionately. It should be big enough to significantly impact your word and the world of those you desire to influence and attract to your organization.

As care givers, connectors and natural networkers, most women find it easy to align with a network marketing company. Once you create your own personal mission statement, ask yourself how it connects with that of your company? Use your mission and that of your company to lead others. People will always follow those individuals who have a clear mission.

Exercise: Creating Your Mission Statement

1. Identify four past successful employments. What areas of those jobs did you enjoy doing and why?

2. Identify four areas/things in your personal life that you believe you excel at. What do you enjoy about them and why?

3. Make a list of the core values that guide your life. Select the top five.

4. Identify ways you would like to give back to your family and community.

5. Identify a list of 50 goals you would like to achieve within the next 5 years. Once you have created your list, sort them into the following areas: financial, business, health, relationship, personal and contribution. Do you see a common theme?

When you have completed each question, highlight the statements that impact you emotionally. Now begin to write a mission statement that is two to three sentences.

Once you have written your mission statement, share it with five people. Ask them to give you feed back on the goals, beliefs, values and overall philosophy reflected in your mission statement.

MLM WOMAN TIP # 6:

Creating a Vision Worthy of Your Life

BY SUSAN

"As you become clearer about who you really are, you'll be better able to decide what is best for you - the first time around."

Oprah Winfrey

What if you started a journey and didn't know your destination? How would you know what clothes to bring, what supplies to pack or even how long you would be away? Chances are whether it is a week's holiday or an outing to the store – you know exactly where you are going.

When I got started in MLM I had a clear focus. I knew exactly where I wanted to be and my first goal was to make $10,000/month. I understood that with a $10,000/month lifestyle I could provide for my family, choose private schools and save for my children's education. The whole notion of the $10,000/month lifestyle and the choices it provided became so consuming that I knew I just had to achieve it.

Many people get started in network marketing and lack a clear vision. They do not even know what they want to achieve with their business. Unfortunately the business often ends up like a hobby. To be truly successful you must have a vision worthy of your life.

I have found the best way to create a vision statement is to write a letter to yourself one year in the future. Describe in detail how you are feeling, where you are living, the car you are driving and every detail you can imagine. Women and men achieve greatness in their multilevel marketing businesses all the time so why not you?

Writing the vision statement in the present, as though everything has already happened, is ideal. This signals to your brain that your dreams are possible. You do not have to know how it is going to happen; you simply must focus on what you want to happen.

If you want people to follow you it is imperative that you know where you are going. No one wants to follow a leader without a clear cut vision. One of the things that attracted many leaders to me was that I had a vision to co-create twenty-five six and multiple six figure women. Living out that vision was what made me a millionaire. Your clear vision can also help you live the life of your dreams.

Exercise: Writing a Letter to Yourself

Write a letter to yourself and date it one year in the future. Describe all of the wonderful things your life includes. Go into detail and write as though it has already happened. Keep this vision statement in a place where you can read it at least once every day.

MLM WOMAN TIP # 7:

Setting up Your Office
BY SUZAN

*"Luck is what happens when preparation
meets opportunity."*

Unknown

One of the first physical steps you will take to establish your home based business is to set up an office. An office is a quiet space in your home where you consistently go to produce. A space that unconsciously lets you and everyone in your life knows it's game time. You are now open for business.

Your office does not have to be fancy or elaborate, it could be a table and chair in a quiet corner of a room. When I first began my business, my office was in a small desk in the corner of our family study. Susan Sly built a multiple six figure income working from a small desk in her young son's bedroom. It is not the size of your office, the real question is does your office have the equipment to allow you to run a successful enterprise?

Your office is your place to dream and produce, so make it your own. Have the pictures on the walls inspire you. Select a screen saver that reflects one of your dreams.

Women are most often responsible for the running of the home. As a result, having an office in your home can be challenging. Teach your family to respect your office space. Set guidelines that help your family understand what you require in order to effectively produce in your space.

When I first established my office, my family was in the habit of calling for me from some other part of the house. They would call, getting louder and louder if I did not answer. As you can imagine this was distracting and unprofessional, as this behavior usually occurred while I was in the middle of a call. I soon had to request that anyone who needed to speak to me must come to my office and wait until I completed my call. This simple request solidified my office hours in the mind of every family member.

Exercise: Setting Up a Productive Office

Below is a list of items and equipment needed to run an efficient, professional and productive office. Schedule a time to set up and personalize your office. Review the list below and confirm the items you already posses. Set a date to acquire any missing items.

1. Computer & printer
    Yes [ ]   No [ ]   Date:_____

2. Professional email address
    Yes [ ]   No [ ]   Date:_____

3. Wireless phone and headset
    Yes [ ]   No [ ]   Date:_____

4. Separate phone line
    Yes [ ]   No [ ]   Date:_____

5. Effective long distance plan
    Yes [ ]   No [ ]   Date:_____

6. Professional voice mail message
    Yes [ ]   No [ ]   Date:_____

7. A full length mirror
   Yes [ ]   No [ ]   Date:_____

8. Clear filing system
   Yes [ ]   No [ ]   Date:_____

9. Business tools; CDs, DVDs, newspapers, magazines and pamphlets
   Yes [ ]   No [ ]   Date:_____

10. A contact manager: computer, index card, note book
    Yes [ ]   No [ ]   Date:_____

11. Book case
    Yes [ ]   No [ ]   Date:_____

12. Bulletin board
    Yes [ ]   No [ ]   Date:_____

13. A vision board
    Yes [ ]   No [ ]   Date:_____

14. Your mission statement
    Yes [ ]   No [ ]   Date:_____

15. Your 12 month vision
    Yes [ ]   No [ ]   Date:_____

16. Educational CDs and books
    Yes [ ]   No [ ]   Date:_____

Know Your Product

BY SUSAN

"Maturity includes the recognition that no one is going to see anything in us that we don't see in ourselves. Stop waiting for a producer. Produce yourself."

Marianne Williamson-author

Imagine going to a store to buy a computer and asking some very basic questions of the sales associate. Instead of answering your questions, a blank look crosses her face and she replies, "I don't know. Here is the phone number of my manager. Why don't you call her and get back to me." You leave, questions unanswered with no intention of calling the manager and instead go to another computer store to purchase your new machine.

If you think that scenario is ridiculous, think again. In my years of network marketing I have had team members who fail to ever learn anything about their products and instead defer their potential clients to their up line for answers. This disqualifies the associate as a leader and also loses the sale. Knowing your product is essential.

The first step in truly knowing your product is to use it yourself and create an emotionally charged story around it. If you are with a company that sells nutritionals then be a product of your product and use it every day. People will be attracted to the passion in your voice, which is something you cannot fake. If your company provides a service then use the service and become passionate about it.

The second step is to research your product. Get yourself trained with the resources the company provides. The more you understand what you have, the greater your belief will be. The greater your belief is, the more believable you are. If you are in a company where you do not believe in your products then chances are you are not making the money you desire.

The third and final step is to know your competition. In network marketing many people simply 'bad mouth' their competition without knowing the facts. In doing this you make yourself look ridiculous and also attract people to you who are negative. It is imperative that you educate yourself on the products. When someone comes to you and is weighing the options between your company and another, you will win simply by pointing out logical differences. For example if your company has a drink with 100 active ingredients and your competitor's drink has only 5 then know about it and point it out.

My mentor taught me the importance of understanding other compensation plans. In learning the four key pay structures I was able to quickly see the features and benefits in every plan. Your product is not just your service or a nutritional formula; your product is also your company's compensation plan. Lastly, you are also your product so make sure you engage in the daily development of yourself.

MLM WOMAN TIP # 9:
Developing Your Story
BY SUZAN

"A bird doesn't sing because it has an answer, it sings because it has a song."

Maya Angelou

When I began my network marketing careers, one of our mentors would continuously use the adage "facts tell and stories sell." As I learned the ropes of the industry I soon realized that people are rarely inspired by facts, rather they are most often moved to seek out more information if they first hear a story that moves and inspires them.

One of the most productive skills you will want to master is the ability to tell your story. This is the art of telling a story in less than 60 seconds, while creating such curiosity, it compels the person hearing the story to ask you for more. A master storyteller knows that the story is not the presentation, rather it is a way of connecting, compelling another to request more information thus creating an opportunity for you to leave a tool, get their contact information and set a time to follow up.

Women are natural storytellers. We can't help but share an experience that has positively impacted our lives. As you learn the art of telling your story allow the listener to connect with your emotion and excitement. Learn to share your story with the same energy you would if you were talking to a close friend.

All compelling stories begin with a personal experience. So in order to develop your story, you must first become a product of your company's product, thus building your belief in your products and or service. Your next step is to learn how to build a short yet powerful story based on your experience.

Exercise: Building Your 60 Second Story

Below is an outline for building your story. Answer each question, writing no more than 3 sentences.

Before your product or service:

1. Context: What was life like before you were introduced to your product?

2. Impact: How did the context impact your life?

3. Feeling: How did the situation make you feel?

Introduction to your product and/or service: by whom and when?

After using your product or service:

1. Context: What is life like after your product and/or service?

2. Impact: How does this new context impact your life?

3. Feeling: How does your new situation make you feel?

Once you have written your story, practice it in front of a mirror. Practice until you are able to deliver you story naturally and with passion. If you are a multiple product company, practice short stories for the various products.

As your business grows, repeat the same process and create your business story.

Know Your Industry
BY SUSAN

"You can have anything in this world you want, if you want it badly enough and you're willing to pay the price."

Mary Kay Ash

We have discussed the importance of knowing your product and I would have to say that knowing your industry is equally important. People ask me how I got to learn so much about different compensation plans and my response is that I am a student of the industry. One of my mentors taught me that knowing the four main compensation plans would give me an advantage. Over the years it has served me well in both prospecting and being prospected.

The four main plans are:

- The Stair Step Breakaway
- The Uni-Level
- The Matrix
- The Binary

Keep in mind that there are derivatives. Most companies will maintain that they have the best compensation plan in the industry. Often companies will also claim to have a unique plan. Regardless of the claims, all plans stem from these initial four.

I have worked all four compensation plans. I have not had great success with some of them and others have been great. For the purposes of this booklet I will focus only on a few key features of each plan. No matter which type of compensation your company uses, the results you achieve will rely on your efforts.

The Stair Step Breakaway is one of the oldest compensation plans. It was designed before super computers. It is based on the premise that a person sponsors wide on their front line and encourages their leaders to build deep. In this plan there is often a benefit to having a minimum number of 'legs' do a certain amount of volume. If one 'leg' exceeds the up line leader in volume the leader is not always paid on that volume.

The Uni-Level encourages the sponsor to place people on their 'front line.' People are paid usually 5-9 levels deep. Anyone coming in below that depth does not generate volume for the person at the top. The front line usually has a higher percentage payout, for example 25%, whereas the volume paid on the lower levels is less.

The Matrix is designed like a square or rectangle. There is a maximum width and depth to which a person can build. The goal is to fill in the spaces. As people leave, the spaces are replaced with active members.

The binary compensation plan is essentially building two teams. The person at the top is paid on their entire organization to a maximum weekly income. This is one of the relatively newer plans and has been given an unfortunate bad reputation. The truth is that almost every person can sponsor two people and if everyone only sponsors two the team fills out.

It is tempting to jump from company to company in search of the best compensation plan. I suggest that you become a student of the industry first and do your homework. Many compensation plans have a 'flushing' feature where volume flushes back to the company. This usually occurs at a certain depth or if the individual does not meet a sponsorship requirement. A breakaway occurs when a team gains momentum and exceeds their up line at which point this team breaks away and the up line is no longer paid on their volume.

When you are researching a company it is very important to find out how many ways a person can get paid. For example can a person sell at retail or does everyone have to become a 'member' or 'affiliate?' Do you get a website? Is there a team bonus? Is there a sponsorship bonus? Understanding the various ways you can make money is critical to evaluating any compensation plan.

The last key point focuses on integrity. Many companies promise the potential to make millions and yet no one has achieved a million dollar income after years in the business. Is the company promising something that isn't possible or has not proven to be true? If so, take a close look at the opportunity and see what the potential is for you to earn income based on your skills, level of desire and ability to connect with people.

Some great questions to ask about a compensation plan are:

1. How many people do you need to sponsor in order to get paid?
2. How many millionaires are there in the company?
3. How many people are earning a six figure income?
4. How many changes have there been to the compensation plan?
5. Is there a breakaway?
6. When does flushing of volume occur?
7. How many ways are there to get paid?
8. How many legs/teams do you have to build to qualify for the top payout in the company?

MLM WOMAN TIP # 11:
Taking a Posture
BY SUZAN

"One is not born a woman, one becomes one."

Simone de Beauvoir

Posture is an attitude. It is an energy that can be seen, felt and heard in your voice. Posture comes from an absolute belief in your products, company and business opportunity. It is to say to the word, "I have the goose that laid the golden egg." To have posture is to have pride in the industry of network marketing but most importantly it is to have an unshakable belief in your ability to create results and experience success. A true leader has the posture of "I am the leader, others can't help but follow." Posture is a presence, an internal power or strength; it is a way of being.

To have posture when leading a team or prospecting is to have total awareness of how you come to every conversation. It is to use your energy to attract people to your opportunity. Let's take some steps to create your posture.

The Auditory Filter: This is a term coined by my friend Susan Sly. The auditory filter is a consistent, persistent voice in your head that is always available to tell you what you can't do and what you do not know. It is the voice that is always willing to criticize and shower you with limiting feedback. As women our auditory filter seem to focus on some very specific themes: "You are too fat and your hips are too big; you can't lead powerful men, they won't listen to you; you can't trust other women and you definitely can't trust men." Now the source of many of these statements is a book unto itself. To have posture you must learn to shut off your auditory filter, understand the source of the limiting dialogue and replace this chatter with positive, affirming statements.

Physical Appearance & Body Language: How do you present yourself to the world? Are you dressed for success? Is your appearance saying "I have influence!" Are you standing upright with your shoulders back? Do you make eye contact? Do you have a firm handshake? Do you introduce yourself in a manner that says I am present and powerfully in the room? How you carry yourself and the manner in which you interact with others will determine whether they give you their time, attention and respect.

Voice & Energy: Are you energetic, passionate and excited? Do you speak with confidence? Is there power in your voice? Projecting power and energy when speaking is often difficult for some women. Many women will speak in a high pitched voice with the majority of the energy originating from their chest cavity. This makes a woman appear timid, shy and lacking in confidence. True power is available when the energy of your speech originates just bellow you belly button. When you are able to connect to this energy source your voice becomes deeper and has more energy. You present as confident, powerful and successful.

Take Charge: Are you able to lead? In prospecting and team building it is imperative that you demonstrate the confidence to lead a conversation. To lead is to be powerfully present in the conversation. It does not mean to monopolize the conversation. Some of the strongest female leaders I know say few words, however when they speak it is powerful and intentional. To lead a conversation is to gracefully stand your ground, not allowing yourself to be intimidated or bullied by aggressive or at times rude individuals. It is the space you claim in the conversation even when in the presence of powerful men. It is to be able to choose to fully express yourself in all circumstances. To take charge in a conversation is to set limits and demand that everyone treat you and your enterprise with respect.

Treating Your Business Like a Million Dollar Venture

BY SUSAN

"Money is only a tool. It will take you wherever you wish, but it will not replace you as the driver."

Ayn Rand, author

I have often trained, coached and worked with people who want to make a seven figure income in network marketing. The sad truth is that they have $10 habits. In other words they are not treating their business with the respect a million dollar venture deserves. You will never make millions in MLM without discipline and solid habits.

Years ago I gave a talk entitled, "Are you training or are you trying for success?" The premise was that many people 'try' to be successful when they should be 'training.' If you decided to do a marathon, which is 26 miles, you wouldn't just wake up one day and run it. You would get some decent shoes, maybe hire a coach, join a group and build up your endurance. You would start by running a few miles and building up to your longer runs. If you tried to run 26 miles all at once you would likely get frustrated and quit because you were not prepared.

The same holds true in network marketing. Success requires daily disciplines. You cannot get into network marketing and simply try to be a millionaire and quit after a few weeks. Take it from me, becoming a network marketing millionaire requires focus, persistence, humility, facing your fears, being coachable, acting in spite of all else and doing something every day to advance yourself.

Are you treating your business like a serious enterprise? Do you have hours of operation, business cards, a professional email, products for sampling, a professional voicemail and a dedicated space to operate your million dollar venture? Are you attending events, getting on webinars and calls, getting mentored, reading books, listening to training audios, prospecting, hosting trainings and working on your beliefs? If you said 'no' to any one of these things then you are simply trying to be successful and not training.

The difference between a millionaire and someone who is broke is that a millionaire believes she can do it. She has an attitude of success and looks for reasons to succeed and not reasons to fail. A millionaire mentality is also one of responsibility. A millionaire takes one hundred percent ownership for her business. Not only is a millionaire's success a result of her actions, her challenges are too. Get out there and train for your success.

If you want to make a million dollars, have million dollar habits. If you want to make $10, then have $10 habits. Success is about training and not simply trying.   - Susan Sly

MILLION DOLLAR MLM HABITS

Check off all that you currently do and make a separate list of items that you intend to work on starting right away.

- Show up for business meetings and appointments on time.
- Keep a set schedule.
- Have office hours.
- Have a professional voicemail.
- Handle mail only once.
- Have a professional email address.
- Dress for success i.e. neat and tidy in appearance.
- Make eye contact with people.

- Read books on business, finance and your industry.
- Take time daily for personal empowerment.
- Attend conferences and trainings.
- Host trainings.
- Get on conference calls.
- Work with your people.
- Keep a log of your activities.
- Set goals.
- Attend to email within 24 hours.
- Return voicemails within 24 hours.
- Have a full selection of sales tools.
- Keep your receipts filed.
- Have a team of people to advise including an accountant, an attorney and other financial advisors.
- Have a coach or mentor.
- Educate yourself on your competition.

MLM WOMAN TIP # 13:
Prospecting
BY SUZAN

"People are like stained-glass windows. They sparkle and shine when the sun is out, but when the darkness sets in, their true beauty is revealed only if there is a light from within."

Elizabeth Kübler-Ross

Most new networkers view prospecting as an act of convincing, of selling someone a product or service. As a result they see prospecting as difficult, a source of fear, discomfort and stress. They view prospecting as a painful process standing between themselves and the results they desire. The fact is if you do not prospect you will not experience success.

To prospect is actually to connect and share your story with another individual. It is the process of building a relationship. As women we do this with ease all the time. When we find something we like, we excitedly share it with those we care about. To prospect is very much the same; it is to get someone's attention, create interest and eventually have the individual become open to reviewing some information. Prospecting is the art of listening and asking the right questions, questions that create dialogue and enable you to understand how your products, services and opportunity may fulfill a desire or need. Prospecting is the act of enrollment; it is your actions, words and energy that leaves a person inspired by who you are. Let's break down the mechanics of prospecting:

1. **Getting the prospect's attention: "Connecting and creating excitement."**

   In order to effectively connect with a potential customer or business partner you have to be clear on who you desire to connect with. Seek out those individuals who appear available and open. These are most often individuals who will smile, make eye contact and respond genuinely to a "hi, how are you?"

   ➤ Connection:
   Hi, how are you?
   Response: *I'm fine how are you?*

   ➤ Interest creating question:
   Isn't it interesting how you can be the best at your craft and not get paid what you are worth? (Pause and wait for a response)

   ➤ Your story or 30 second commercial:
   Well that was me just a year ago. Then a friend introduced me to this simple business, and now I make more part time that I did when I was working full time. (Pause and wait for a response)

   ➤ Wait for an invitation to present a tool:
   How can I learn more about this business?

2. **Building Interest: "Let the tools do the talking"**

   This is done by presenting your potential customer or business partner with a tool, getting their contact information and setting a specific time to follow up. The tool could be a CD, DVD, pamphlet or sending someone to your company website. It could also be an invitation to have someone listen to a sizzle call or attend a home presentation or hotel event.

   ➤ Offer a tool:
   If you are truly interested, I can loan you the CD I listen to. It takes about 20 minutes. It's actually how I learned about the business. (Pause and wait for a response)

➤ Get their email address:
  Do you have an email I can contact you at? (Pause and wait for a response)

➤ Get their name:
  My name is Cindy Black, what's yours? (Pause and wait for a response)

➤ Set a time to follow up:
  I will call you tonight to find out what you liked best about what you heard. I am available this evening between 6:00 & 7:00 or 7:00 & 8:00, what time works best for you?
  (pause and wait for a response)

➤ Obtain the phone number they will answer at the time of the appointment:
  What phone number will you answer at 7:30?
  (pause and wait for a response)

3. Follow Up: "The fortune is in the follow up."

   During the follow up call your primary goal is to determine your potential customer or business partner level of interest. Here are four simple but effective ways to determine a person's level of interest:

➤ Ask open ended questions :
  What did you like most about what you heard?
  Did you see a benefit for yourself?
  What questions can I get answered for you?

➤ Determine if they are asking "How" questions vs. "Why" questions:

   How question are most often asked when someone is seeking to understand. Why questions usually indicate convince me. Remember you are not in the convincing business.
   How does the compensation plan work?
   I'm skeptical, why should I belief all the stories I heard?

➤ Have them identify their level of interest on a scale of 1 – 10:
  On a scale of 1 – 10, 1 being no interest and 10 being extremely interested, how would you rate you level of interest?

➤ Guideline for Prospecting:

   a. Commit 80% of your time to prospecting
   b. Create 2-3 quality connections a day
   c. Always carry a selection of tools
   d. Keep a small note pad handy
   e. Set an appointment to follow up.
   f. Always get the prospects contact information.
   g. Once you have the prospect contact information, change the topic.
   h. Always ask for referrals.
   i. Be yourself, lead with your heart and have fun

Exercise: The 52 Card Challenge

Like any other business, your skill gets stronger with practice. Contact two team members and practice prospecting and setting a time to follow up. Practice on your own by using the mirror in your newly set up office.

Once you have built some confidence, I invite you to do the 52 Card Challenge with two team member. This Challenge is fun way for you and your team members to get into action and create results. Take a deck of cards and place them face down on your desk. Every time you effectively prospect a potential customer or business partner flip over a card. The first person to go threw the deck of card, wins the challenge. To make the challenge more interesting, track the number of "yes" and "no" you receive.

MLM WOMAN TIP # 14:

The Importance of Using Sales Tools

BY SUSAN

"Luck has nothing to do with it, because I have spent many, many hours, countless hours, on the court working for my one moment in time, not knowing when it would come."

Serena Williams, athlete

In network marketing you are the messenger. The tools are your message. This business is about getting people in front of information and collecting a decision. There are many tools available to you regardless of the company you are in. The fun part is deciding which tool to use and becoming skilled at repetition.

When I first started in network marketing I wanted very badly to be perfect. I thought that people might judge me if I didn't know enough. Instead of using tools such as CDs (in those days audio cassettes), and DVDs (think video tapes,) I did the 'tell and sell' routine. My closing rate was horrible and I realized that the more I tried to deliver the message without using the tools the more I turned people away because they thought they could never do what I did.

Through reading and education I realized that I was stuck. I decided that I was going to talk less and let the tools do the work. I began taking people onto prospecting calls, getting them out to events, having them listen to 24/7 recorded calls, watching DVDs and listening to CDs. My closing rate improved dramatically.

I have signed people up using leads, running ads, post cards, calling people from the phone book, meeting people in restaurants, grocery stores and even Starbucks. I prefer to have people call me and that is why I like ads. However in my lead calling days I was pretty good. When I had a leads list I called the people right away and created a sense of urgency. My initial call was always 'interview style' and involved asking questions such as:

-What has you in a position that you are looking for a home based business?

-Have you ever owned a business before?

-How much money are you looking to make on a monthly basis?

-If money were not an object what would you be doing to design your life?

-If you found the right opportunity would you have money to invest in your own business and get started right away?

-How soon do you want to make a change to start improving your life?

When the person had great energy and a positive attitude I took them onto a live presentation over the phone. If they had a negative attitude I simply thanked them for their time and suggested that owning a business was not for them. It was amazing how people changed when they saw I wasn't desperate.

The tool in this case was the live recruiting call. Instead of me giving the information right there over the phone, I said, "let me take you on a ten minute live presentation with someone making a significant amount of money in this amazing company." What my prospects learned right away was that this business was simply about inviting 'guests' onto a call.

Many companies have 24/7 recorded recruiting calls, websites and other tools that allow you to bring your prospects in front of information right away. Network marketing literally has become a virtual business. Directing your potential clients and business partners to online presentations has completely automated the industry.

For people building in a local market, which for me is anywhere I am local to at that moment, I suggest being prepared. Make sure you are always stocked on your company's materials. Many MLMs have excellent CDs, DVDs, catalogues, magazines, newspapers and other resources. To respect the people you are connecting with it is best to offer a choice.

When I first started in the industry I gave people a package with every tool we had. I later found out that the majority of prospects never looked at the material because the larger the selection the more overwhelming it was. I discovered that simply asking someone what they prefer is the simplest way to get a tool into the hands of your potential partner.

A sample conversation would go something like this:

You: *Don, it really sounds like you are interested in making more money this year.*

Don: *Absolutely.*

You: *Don I have a variety of information suited to your convenience. Would you prefer to listen to something in your car, read something or look at something online?'*

When a person willingly chooses a piece of information they are more likely to review it. We will address closing in MLM Woman Tip # 16. For right now your goal is to be the messenger and get people in front of the message in the form of your tools. Let people come to their own conclusion from the information you are sharing. Ultimately when you have tools in the hands of many people you are more likely to close a few.

Some companies, such as Sound Concepts – www.soundconcepts.com, offer great generic tools with incredible entrepreneurs such as Robert Kiosaki of *Rich Dad Poor Dad* fame. A person with a success minded attitude will stock up on a variety of sales tools and learn to use all of them.

The Ultimate 3–Way Call

BY SUZAN

"No one goes alone to the heights of excellence. Your success will depend on others, and theirs will depend on you."

Unknown

The 3-way call is one of the most powerful skills you will learn as a networker. The 3-way call occurs when you introduce your potential customer or business partner to a credible member of your team. During the call your team member will answer your prospect's questions, provide third party validation of your products, services and business opportunity, while demonstrating to the prospect that you are part of a team and support is readily available.

Here are the steps to build the ultimate 3-way:

1. **Creating Interest:** Before you consider doing a 3-way call you should have captured your prospect's interest by using an interest creating statement or by quickly sharing your product or business story. You will have given your prospect a tool to review and your prospect will have expressed a significant level of interest in your products, service or business opportunity. A great question to evaluate a prospect's interest is to ask, "On a scale of 1 – 10 how excited are you about the information you have just seen?" If your prospect's interest level is a 7 or above they qualify for a 3-way call.

2. **Setting Up a 3-way:** Once you have qualified your prospect for a 3-way call, let them know you are going to set up a call with a leader on your team. Do not ask permission, lead your prospect and present the call as the logical next step. As you are setting up the 3-way call, take a few moments to edify the leader that is going to do the call.

    To edify is to give a brief description of the leader's experience, skills and successes. It is to have your prospect believe they are going to be connected to an expert, someone who has achieved or is in the process of achieving the results they desire. While edifying your leader do not tell their story as that is frequently used by the leader to open the 3-way call and connect with the prospect. When selecting a leader to do your 3-way call, choose an individual who may have a similar background, interest or experience as your prospect. This will help your prospect feel that the leader on the line can identify with them and effectively answer their questions.

    Example: *"We are going to be speaking with Susan Sly. Susan is a trainer for our company. Susan is a nutritionist and a world class athlete. She is also a stay at home mom. Susan built her multiple six figure income while at home raising her children. I know Susan will be able to answer your questions."*

3. **Setting the Time:** Once you have presented the 3-way call, obtain 2 -3 possible times from your prospect. Now connect with your leader and confirm a time.

4. **Beginning the 3-way Call:** Contact your leader about five minutes before the 3-way call. At this time you will want to give your leader information about your prospect and some insight into the possible questions they may want answered. Once you have briefed your leader, dial your prospect number and link the call.

5. **Introducing Your Leader:** The next step is to introduce your prospect to your leader. This is done by edifying your leader once again. During the introduction you do not edify the prospect. This subtle but effective tactic will continue to subconsciously give your prospect the image that they are meeting someone influential.

6. **Your Silence Is Golden:** When your prospect answers the phone, confirm that it is still a good time to do the call and introduce your leader. The introduction must occur within the first 60 seconds of the call. Once you have completed your introduction your role is complete. You do not speak unless invited back into the conversation by your leader. If you speak after you have handed over the call, you actually begin to discredit your leader. You are subconsciously conveying the message "I am not confident in this leader, so I am going to jump into the conversation to ensure they don't miss anything."

7. **Leave It in Your Leader's Capable Hands:** Once you have turned the call over to your leader, she will complete the following steps:

   ➤ Create a connection: This is often done by having the prospect share their goal and what they saw that excited them. The leader will also use this time to share her story.

   ➤ Answer question: She answers the questions the prospect has.

   ➤ Paint a picture: The leader will enroll the prospect in the possibility that their "why" can be obtained by embarking on this journey.

   ➤ Getting started: The leader will walk the prospect through what it will take to get started.

   ➤ Collect a decision: The leader will ask for the sale and obtain an address, personal information and a method of payment.

8. **Completing the registration:** Once the method of payment is established, your leader will turn the call back over to you to complete the registration and set up the next call.

   For a 3-way to be effective it is imperative that you trust the skills and expertise of the leader doing the call. The leader will assess if this person is a good candidate or if it is best to end the call. If the leader chooses to end the call, the expectation is that you follow her lead. It is often tempting for the new associate to begin talking after the leader has chosen to let the prospect go. Again this diminishes the credibility of the leader and demonstrates to the prospect that you are willing to partner with anyone.

Exercise: Setting Up a Powerful 3-Way Call

1. Make a list of leaders in your company you respect and have a desire to do 3-way calls with. Contact them and find out their business hours. Obtain a small bio and write a short introduction for each leader.

2. Ensure your phone has 3-way capabilities and practice linking a third person onto the line. It is also valuable to practice disconnecting from a 3-way call.

3. Practice greeting your prospect and edifying your leader within the first 60 seconds of the call.

4. If you are tempted to talk during a 3-way call, place a role of duct tape on your desk by the phone as a friendly reminder.

Closing the Deal

BY SUSAN

"I don't think a tough question is disrespectful."

Helen Thomas, journalist

In network marketing it is critical to collect decisions and these come in the form of 'yes' or 'no.' We get paid dollars to collect 'yes' answers, however, the payment for the word 'no' comes in the form of education, which is priceless. Either way, a few 'yes' answers will make you; a few 'no's will merely challenge you.

Many women fear rejection and that is why they do not close. That one simple word 'no' is enough to terrify the strongest gal. Because of this fear, it becomes easier to have a lot of people looking at your information and very few making a decision. Closing is the key difference between a hobby and a successful venture. When you master it, you want to do it all day long. When you fear it, you want to avoid it all day long.

Closing, very simply, is a dance. There is a logical progression from creating an I.G.R. or interest generating remark, to trial closing once or twice, to finally asking for the sale. Very few people actually ask for the sale. The number one reason people buy anything is because they are asked.

Have you ever gone to a store with an intention to 'look' and found yourself walking out with something other than the item you went to look at? We all have. More than likely someone approached you with a sample, a coupon or a suggestion that lead you to tasting or trying something on and the 'dance' was over and you purchased. Your network marketing business is no different. The faster you embrace closing and collecting the decisions, the faster you will move forward.

When a person has expressed interest in your opportunity or product it is essential to get them in front of information. If you are in a nutritional company you may also have them try a sample. If you are in a skin care company you may do a demonstration to illustrate the effectiveness of the product. By having a person sample your product or service they are more likely to buy and this is a form of trial closing.

Have you ever purchased a new car? Perhaps you went to the dealership intending only to buy a certain model that was within your budget. The next thing you know you are test driving a luxury model and your budget car no longer seems adequate. This is all part of a trial close – having a person experience the product.

If you are working with people at a distance, the trial close involves presenting information and asking a direct question such as, 'from the information you have seen, what has captivated you the most?' From there a great closing question is, 'what further questions can I get answered in order for you to make a decision to get started today?'

When a person is asking questions that are specific it is a good idea to introduce third party validation in the form of a 3-way phone call. If you do not have an up line member to do a 3-way call with then simply ask a person what further information they require. This is why we encourage you to know your product. When questions arise, and they will, you are easily able to point someone in the right direction.

When it comes to closing, people like to be lead. Very few people can actually make decisions for themselves and this is why mass media uses celebrities and actors impersonating physicians to sway the audience. Consumers have become savvier, however they are still influenced by people who they feel can lead them to something desirable.

A great way to lead into the close is to ask the person which flavor they prefer, for example chocolate or vanilla. Which credit card they will be using or where they would like their product shipped. People will realize they are being closed, however when they hear the posture in your voice, they will be more likely to follow.

The first few times I lead people to a close in network marketing I was literally sweating and my pulse was racing. The more closing I did, the more comfortable I became. To grow into a successful leader in MLM you will learn to take a posture with people and collect that 'yes' or 'no' answer.

I would encourage you to visit your pipeline and go collect some decisions. Remember, the only way to fail is not to try at all. Becoming a master closer is simply a matter of mass repetition. Even the best closers in the world encounter rejection. The difference is that they never take it personally; they simply go on to the next person until they get their 'yes.'

The most successful entrepreneurs are constantly prospecting and closing whether it is to get a better deal or better service. The millionaires I know, myself included, practice closing every day. We consider it an essential aspect of our success.

CLOSING NUMBERS TO CONSIDER

1. It takes the average person 5-7 exposures before they buy.

2. Only about 1-3% of people will say 'yes' on the first approach.

3. Of the people you close, about 80% will be product users.

4. Of the remaining 20% you close, only about 3% will build the business with little or no assistance.

5. Successful networkers are constantly closing as practice tends to make perfect.

Your Pipeline

BY SUZAN

"I knew what my job was; it was to go out and meet the people and love them."

Princess Diana

A pipeline is a list of individuals you desire to contact about your products, services and business opportunity. These names may come from your warm market, recent contact from your community as well as referral from customers, business associates and friends.

To effectively prospect you require more names than you have time. Imagine if your pipeline consisted of 10 names. Once you received 5 "no" answers, you would become attached to the outcome. You would begin to come from a place of desperation thinking, "I only have 5 names left and I have not gotten a yes. Chances are these thoughts would change your energy on the call, making you come across desperate and willing to partner with anyone.

Now imagine you have a list of 200 names. A no will definitely not have the same impact. Kathy Smith, a network marketing millionaire taught me that every no brings me closer to my next yes. I learned that when my pipeline was full and I was in action, a no really just meant not now.

FILLING YOUR PIPELINE

To avoid the feeling of desperation, and to maintain a high level of prospecting, it is important to continuously replenish your pipeline. Below is a list of ways to consistently filter names into you pipeline:

1. Always ask for referrals

2. Invite existing customers to host home presentations

3. Request a list of 10 referrals from every customer

4. Attend networking events

5. Join a network group

6. Take successful people to lunch and ask for their help

7. Purchase leads

8. Run ads

9. Begin a paper route

10. Leave pamphlets or brochures at the offices of other professionals

Another great way to fill your pipeline is what is known as the "walk and talk" or the "three foot rule." This is to connect with every open, positive person who comes within three feet of you. When you become comfortable with the "three foot rule," you can prospect as you are running your daily errands, while taking your children to their activities or even when doing your shopping. When I am getting my nails or hair done it is often the best time to prospect. Imagine a group of women with nothing but time on their hands while they wait for their services. With this approach even the busiest women can always find opportunities to prospect. Often the busier you are, the easier it becomes to prospect.

For the "three foot rule" to be effective, you must master your story and practice a number of interest creating statements. An effective way to engage in a conversation with someone is to ask leading questions using FORM. This acronym stands for Family, Occupation, Recreation and Money. When you get a prospect to openly talk about themself and you use leading questions, you can easily discover how your products, service and business opportunity may be of assistance.

THE 24 – 48 HOUR TURN AROUND

A great way to ensure that prospects are consistently being moved through your pipeline is the 24-48 hour turn around. This simply is a commitment to follow up with a prospect within 48 hours of giving them information. This method, when used effectively, has you provide information, follow up and complete a 3-way while the energy and excitement from the initial connection is still present. If you wait much longer than 48 hours you may have to go back and begin the process from the beginning. Commit to continuously move prospects through your pipeline. If you find a prospect has been in your pipeline for more than a week have a "fence kicking party." This simply means, make it your priority to shake the fence and collect a decision.

SEVEN EXPOSURES

If a prospect is not interested in your opportunity do not get discouraged and write them off. Use your contact manager, file their information and set a date to reconnect with them within 1 to 3 months. Network marketing is often about timing. The average prospect needs to be exposed to information at least seven times before they are able to make an informed decision.

Exercise: The 24 – 48 Hour Turn Around

Create a list of 30 prospects. Mount their names on a large post it on your office wall. Begin to contact each individual with the goal of getting their attention, creating interest and setting a time to follow up. Set your time to follow up within the first 24 hours of your initial call. Commit to creating a 3-way call and collecting a decision within 48 hours. As you collect decisions, move the prospect's name out of your pipeline and replace it with a new name. Your goal is to always have 30 names in your pipeline and to move each prospect through a process as quickly as possible. Have fun, be bold and play at 100%.

"Activity creates the space for true learning" -Suzan Hart

MLM WOMAN TIP # 18:

How to Build and Develop Your Team

BY SUSAN

"I am a big believer that eventually everything comes back to you. You get back what you give out."

Nancy Reagan

There have been numerous books written on leadership and management. Network marketing requires a variety of skills when it comes to team building and I suggest you read books such as John C. Maxwell's *Developing the Leader Within* and Donald Trump's *Think Big and Kick Ass* to further explore what it takes to lead. At Step into Your Power we offer a course called Empowered Leadership, which assists people in identifying their leadership style and overcoming their fears when it comes to positions of influence.

Building a team in network marketing is going to pull from you every joy and every fear possible. There will be days when you think that you are invincible and other days when you want to turn off the phone and crawl under the covers. True team builders regulate their energy and resist the temptation of 'highs' and 'lows' and I would encourage you to do the same. It wasn't until I stopped taking things personally that I began to create results. Team building required dealing with a range of personality types and using diplomacy with all of them. Some of your team members may love you while others blame their lack of success on you. Either way, you must stay strong and consistent.

Some of the personalities that may emerge on your team are:

Type A - Aggressor
This person knows what she wants and isn't afraid to use influence to get it. This person requires very little motivation and tends to be an 'island' i.e. they have an 'I can do it all by myself' attitude.

Type B – Believer
This person believes in what they are doing and will need to borrow from your belief. This person will have hot and cold days. They are mostly positive though sometimes they may come across as needy.

Type C – Care Giver
This person is more interested in helping people so that they will be liked than they are in working on themselves. They are often very nice people and you will spend a lot of emotional energy trying to motivate them to build a business.

Type D – Destroyer
This person has negative energy and blames their lack of success on everyone and everything else. They can poison your team so you will want to keep them contained.

People can be a combination of any one or more of these traits. Knowing that you will encounter all types is part of taking on the honor of leadership. People will not respect you by what you say; they will respect you by what you do. In the course of my network marketing career I have had people say that I became a millionaire by luck when in reality it was diligent work.

One of my mentors shared with me that the secret to her success was matching energy with people. I learned that I could only put into people as much as they were willing to give in return. I have witnessed many women become exhausted in this industry because they were trying to motivate people who were not contributing back. In reality, energy can neither be created nor destroyed. When you are pouring all of your energy into someone and spending time with the negative people, your energy will shift and your results will suffer.

Team building requires identifying the people who are asking the right questions. Potential leaders ask 'how' questions. Energy drainers and negative people ask 'why' questions. There is a huge difference between someone who asks, 'how do I grow my team,' versus someone who asks, 'why isn't this working?'

In order to effect change you must do whatever you want your team to do. If you want to work with positive people then become one. If you want people to do events and take charge then do it yourself. If you want people to be open then work on being open. You must focus your energy on the people that are willing to work. A great rule to apply to team building is to focus 80% of your energy on the 20% of the people who will produce 80% of your paycheck.

Many teams have a handful of toxic people. These people can really undo a lot of the good you are doing. The best advice is to have a clearing conversation with them and ask them if they are willing to move forward with a positive attitude. If the answer is 'no' then silently bless them, wish them well and do not focus there.

MLM WOMAN TIP # 19:
Giving the Ultimate Presentation
BY SUZAN

"Words mean more than what is set down on paper. It takes the human voice to infuse them with deeper meaning."

Maya Angelou

A presentation is an event where you provide information to an individual or group. All effective presentation has a predetermined timeline, a clear purpose and a desired outcome. There are three types of presentations:

a) *One on One:* This is a presentation to one prospect. It can occur in person or on the telephone.

b) *An in Home:* This is a presentation to a small group. It most often occurs in your home or the home of a prospect or team member.

c) *Large Group:* This is a presentation to 40 or more individuals. This type of presentation can often occur at a hotel or hall. It is most often an opportunity for associates to invite prospects to learn about a company's products and business. A large group presentation is often hosted by a local leader or an invited guest.

Start with the End in Mind: When hosting a presentation it is important to prepare with a clear intention and desired outcome. Below are some great questions to assist in your planning:

a) Who is my audience?
b) What is the purpose of this presentation?
c) What is my desired outcome?
d) What lesson or information do I desire to provide?

Practice: Once you have decided on the purpose, outcome and content of your presentation, take time to prepare notes and a simple outline. Use your notes to prepare and practice. Practice until you begin to feel comfortable with the information. Practice until you are able to use your outline as a guide and are no longer dependent on your notes. This will enable you to connect with the audience.

Keep It Simple: Although most companies have an array of data, statistics and studies that are highly beneficial, your responsibility as a presenter is to provide the audience with enough information to allow them to make an informed decision. Your role is to provide a simple, timely presentation that addresses some key questions:

a) What is it?
b) Why does it work?
c) Where did it come from?
d) Is it safe?
e) What did it do for you?
f) What did it do for others?
g) Will it do the same for me?
h) How much does it cost?

Be Prepared: When planning any presentation, ensure you have the necessary supplies.

This is a list of frequently used supplies:

a) Product & product display
b) Registration forms
c) Presentation binders
d) DVD player
e) DVD or power point

f) Television
g) Projector
h) Lap top
i) A screen
j) Microphone & audio equipment
k) Pens
l) Paper
m) Name tags
n) Bottled water
o) Registration table

Be Compliant: The network marketing industry is governed by a series of rules and regulations. As a result, when planning your presentation ensure your presentation is approved by your company and is free of claims. When using testimonials, meet with each speaker prior to your presentation to ensure their statements are compliant.

Credibility & Integrity: As a presenter you represent your company and associates, so how you present yourself is of the utmost importance. Be respectful to your audience at all times. Conduct yourself with integrity, as your credibility and that of your team can be lost by one inappropriate statement or by presenting misinformation. If asked a question you are unsure of do not give misinformation. Commit to finding the answer and informing the audience or prospect at a future date.

Questions: When doing a group or home presentation it is best to handle question on a one to one basis. A highly successful presentation can fall apart while a presenter attempts to answer a question from a skeptical and sometimes difficult prospect. It is best to close the presentation and inform the audience that the presenter and leaders will be available to answer any questions after the presentation.

Respect Time: It is important that all presentations have a predetermined timeline. When hosting a presentation be respectful of your guests and start and end on time. An effective presentation runs from one hour to an hour and thirty minutes.

Environment: When giving a presentation the environment can often make or break an event. For a one on one presentation, select a quiet location where you and the prospect can easily concentrate. Request that your prospect is able to give you their full attention. If a prospect appears distracted or rushed, it may be in your best interest to reschedule. Remember timing is everything.

For a home presentation, it is most often the host that is responsible for creating the environment. Recommend that your host greet and introduce the guests to one another. Playing light background music and directing your guest to a well laid out product display can often create discussion and excitement. When possible have samples available for your guests to try. As this interaction is occurring, encourage associates who are in the room to share their 60 second story.

At a group event, every individual involved is responsible for creating a fun and welcoming environment. This includes the associates at the registration desk, the greeters at the door and finally the host and presenters. Upbeat music can be used to create and raise the energy and excitement in the room. As in the home party, encourage associates to share their excitement and introduce their guests to the presenter and other leaders in the room.

When choosing a room, select a room that will effectively accommodate the number of expected guest. It is better to have a small room full to capacity than a large, empty room. The temperature of a room is also very important to the success of a presentation. A warm, stuffy room will cause your audience to become tired and lethargic. Set the room temperature somewhat cool yet not cold and uncomfortable.

The Introduction: When doing any presentation, it is imperative to set the tone. This can be accomplished by introducing yourself and powerfully sharing your product and business story with the audience.

Similar to the 3-way call, the introduction of the speakers that follow is of absolute importance. The host is responsible for edifying and introducing each speaker. Again, remember not to share the speaker's story as this is how most speakers will connect with the audience and earn their right to present on their assigned topic.

Engage the Audience: The most powerful and fun presentations are those where the audience gets to participate. A gifted presenter is not necessarily the most informed, rather it is the individual who is able to connect and create dialogue with the audience. When planning your presentations we invite you to find creative ways to involve your audience. Here are a few examples:

a) Ask enrolling questions
b) Get the audience to raise their hands to indicate agreement
c) Ask for and prepare testimonials
d) Recognition & door prizes

Have Fun: One of the most important yet frequently overlooked components of a presentation is fun. Ensure your events are fun and able to capture the audience. Get creative, use humor and plan fun activities to engage the audience.

MLM WOMAN TIP # 20:

Setting and Getting Goals
BY SUSAN

*"Do the one thing you think you cannot do. Fail at it. Try
again. Do better the second time. The only people who
never tumble are those who never mount the high wire.
This is your moment. Own it."*

Oprah Winfrey

Goal setting is one of the most important things you will do in your
network marketing business. It is a relatively simple task and yet very
few people actually set specific goals usually for fear that they are
not realistic or achievable. Goals do not have to be realistic. In fact,
in Napoleon Hill's classic tome – *Think and Grow Rich,* Hill says that
your mind would not fathom something unless it was possible.

Setting goals is a great way to mark your progress. Ideally you should
set goals that are reasonable and goals that will stretch you. If you are
currently making $1000/month in your business then set a goal to
make $2000/month and beyond. When you achieve a smaller goal it
gives you the confidence to go for larger, more meaningful goals.

I keep a goal book. Currently, while we are putting together this
book, there are 1000 goals listed. Whenever I am on an airplane and
sometimes before bed I will write out new goals. Some of the goals

have already been achieved. When you begin to write your goals, and I would recommend starting with one hundred, you will be amazed at how soon they start to come true.

When I achieve a goal I write 'victory' in large letters beside it. There is something greatly satisfying about knowing that I have already achieved my dreams. You can do this too and it is never too late to get started with writing down your goals, dreams and desires.

Some simple tips for writing goals are:

- Write a goal in the present for example: I am earning $100,000/year in my network marketing business.
- Write a goal that is focused on the positive and not the negative. For example: I am 100% cash positive versus I am getting out of debt.
- Write goals that have meaning for you.
- Write goals that are specific. For example instead of saying – I live in a new house – describe that house to the smallest detail.
- Write the goals that you describe in your vision statement.
- Write goals that encompass all areas of your life including health, finance, relationships, giving back, fun and education. For example if there is a course or seminar you wish to take then write that as one of your goals. If you want to be a different size then write that too.

Creating goals is something that has always brought me great joy. Seeing these goals manifest is extremely satisfying.

I was once doing a seminar in Philadelphia with my great friend Jeffrey Combs. I was delivering a piece on *Goal Getting Mastery*, one of our Step into Your Power programs, and asked the audience what they wanted. Mary*, one of the women seemed extremely upset by my question so I went up to her and said, 'Mary - what do you want?' She began to sob. She said, 'for the last fifteen years no one has ever asked me what I want. I am so busy making lunches, doing homework and laundry that I have forgotten to even focus on me.' She had a huge breakthrough that day.

Women are such great givers and not always the best receivers. To become a goal getting master it is critical that you learn to set goals,

78

focus in and be ready for them when they come. A great example of not being ready is the staggering statistic of lottery winners. Over 90% of all people who win the lottery lose their money in the first few years. They focused on winning, got into action by purchasing the ticket and then were unprepared when it came. For every goal you set it is imperative that you educate yourself along the way by reading books on finance, health and relationships so when the abundance comes you are ready and capable of sustaining it.

In my goal book I also write items of gratitude as I am grateful for everything I already have. In doing this I feel more peaceful and fulfilled. It is a great exercise. Additionally I cannot emphasize enough the importance of writing out at least ten items of gratitude every single day. This will keep things in perspective. Being grateful for the smallest things and even the challenges life throws our way signals that we are ready for bigger and better things.

The best time to start writing your goals is now. Suzan and I encourage you to post them in your office space. You may even want to create a vision board with pictures and phrases that inspire you. I have a portable one for when I travel and a larger one in a prominent place in my office. I am constantly visualizing my goals.

At Step into Your Power we teach a simple six step system for achieving your goals.

1. Figure out what you absolutely do not want.
2. Replace that with what you want.
3. Take time daily to visualize achieving that goal.
4. Get into the feeling place of already having attained the goal.
5. Get into action and let go of the results – they will take care of themselves.
6. Take time daily to be thankful for what you already have.

30 Day Goals

1. _____
2. _____
3. _____
4. _____
5. _____

60 Day Goals

1. _____
2. _____
3. _____
4. _____
5. _____

90 Day Goals

1. _____
2. _____
3. _____
4. _____
5. _____

6 Month Goals

1. _____
2. _____
3. _____
4. _____
5. _____

1 Year Goals

1. _____
2. _____
3. _____
4. _____
5. _____

Real Women, Real Success

REALIZING YOUR POTENTIAL AND LIVING YOUR DREAMS

When I entered law school back in 1979, I did so with the aspirations of taking over the family business. My life took one of many unexpected turns when in my third year, my father was in financial trouble and sold the business. I soon found myself practicing matrimonial law for at least 60 hours a week. It was an extremely stressful job filled with both gratification and heartache.

I became pregnant and was very much looking forward to my maternity leave, I needed the break. It was a shock to discover that my son was born with a severe health challenge and consequently leaving work was not an option. I became very involved fundraising related to my son's health challenge, which I very much enjoyed but for personal reasons I later had to step back.

In 1993 I had a beautiful daughter and in 1995 I re-entered the work force. I began a company called Orthotic Solutions fitting people with custom made orthotics. The company grew quite large and I was soon one of the largest providers in the field. It was a very lucrative endeavor but not one I found fulfilling. Fortunately, in 2004, I was introduced to products that were marketed via network marketing. I fell in love with both the products and the industry. Not only is the industry providing a six figure income to my family, it is providing to me a feeling of purpose, which, as a baby boomer, I had been looking for.

I feel now, as I approach 50, that I have truly been blessed with a wonderful and supportive family and a new career that is truly helping people improve both their health and financial well being. Network marketing empowers everyone to realize their potential and live their dreams. How wonderful it is to be a part of that.

Susan Bernstein
Thornhill, Ontario

CONVERTED TO NETWORK MARKETING

I have been aware of network marketing virtually all of my life but was not drawn to it for years. In fact I had quite the aversion to it, but that all changed for me when I fell in love with a product and found the right company for me..

I was a single mom with 3 young children, and I was reluctant to go back to teaching school, which is really the only formal training I had. So with the need to make ends meet, and the desire to keep my home, I signed a teaching contract even though I really did not want to go back to teaching. A few weeks before school started I stumbled upon my network marketing opportunity and I felt like this was something that I wanted to do. I fell in love with the product and my perspective changed when I realized that network marketing is simply people who are so excited about a product or an opportunity that they can't keep it to themselves. It is a magnetic thing that creates residual business.

Within 12 months of starting with the company, my group was doing $1.4 million in sales. I didn't have any previous experience, I didn't have any capital to start a new business; I did, however, have passion and am a quick learner. I did trade shows and invited people to my home. Within less than a year I was making in single months more than I would have made in an entire year teaching school. I made my first million dollars by the time I was 35. Now, 18 years later, I have a couple hundred thousand people in my team worldwide and have as much heart for the business as ever. I really learned the value of residual income when I had my fourth child and decided to temporarily retire and devote all my energy to family for 18 months.

As a result of my previous efforts, my check never fell below $15,000 a month during that time. What a gift!

The perk for me is that I am able to travel the world with my kids. I made a promise to them early on that if they would support me in being away from home more than I wanted to be in those early years that someday I would take them everywhere I would go. They have now been to China, Japan, Malaysia, Singapore, and Thailand; they have been all over Eastern and Western Europe, Egypt, Greece, México, and to Alaska many times. I just got back from Kazakhstan, Uzbekistan and Siberia. Who would have guessed that I would have a business where virtually all of Eastern Europe and Southeast Asia are in my down line? Even though I was away in some of those earlier days, the freedom the business has given me to take a week or a month off, to stop my day to read my children a story or go to a game, has been a tremendous gift. Network marketing has made such a difference in other people's lives, in my children's lives and in my own life that I cannot even put a price on it.

Margie Aliprandi
Utah, USA

FINANCIAL SECURITY

I am a passionate and energetic woman. My husband Adrian and I are from the land of blue skies & sunshine, acres of palm trees — paradise — Glendale, Arizona. We enjoy the lifestyle that working from home affords us. We love being able to travel where and when we want and enjoy our 5 children, their spouses and our 15 grandchildren.

I have been in the network marketing industry for the last 18 years. I don't know of a more lucrative profession that affords the time, freedom, and joy in helping others succeed than this industry.

I was lucky enough to be a stay-at-home mom while raising my five children. After I put my youngest one in school, I was ready to do something for myself, for my personal growth. I took up tennis, and then opened up a tennis shop/boutique. It was during this time I was introduced to network marketing. I had always avoided getting involved with network marketing. (Being from Utah, the home of nearly 200 network marketing companies, I had been approached a lot over the years and never thought it was right for me.) Someone introduced me to a product and I knew my three sisters, cousins and some of my friends would love it too. I started sharing it with my friends and family and before I knew it, I was making more with my part-time network marketing than I was in my pro shop. My husband didn't like the idea of it, but said that it could be my little extra spending money. He said I just couldn't talk to any of the neighbors, people at his work, or anyone at Church. Within two or three years of working hard and building my networking business, I had doubled and almost tripled my husband's income he'd worked 30 years to build.

Tragedy struck our family when my 48 year-old husband was diagnosed with prostate cancer and within sixteen months, he was gone. I had lost my sweetheart to cancer! Life is so fragile. None of us has any guarantees or knows when tragedy might strike. I still had several kids at home, and what started out to be my "Plan B" soon turned into my "Plan A." We had always thought, "When the kids are gone, we will get out of debt." We never had that opportunity.

I have learned first hand the benefits of leveraging and residual income. I don't know what profession or job I could have started that would have given me the time off to be home where I needed and wanted to be, and would have kept paying me week after week, month after month. Those checks were in my mailbox and actually increasing each week. It's about teamwork and leverage. I had worked hard to build a team and what I had set in motion, carried in motion. As hard as it was losing my husband, financially my family and I were OK.

Are you willing to pay the price to live your dreams? Everything comes with a price tag; you get what you pay for in this business. It's the people who stay committed and focused who will reap the rewards of a true residual income. You have to be persistent, consistent, focused and driven. There is nothing sweeter than seeing the people you're working with reach their full potential. I have always believed that if you help enough people get what they want, you can have anything you want. Success follows when people come first.

Janiell Vashon
Arizona, USA

I NOW EMBRACE AN INDUSTRY I USED TO HATE

I always hated multilevel marketing . . . call it what you may: network marketing, relationship marketing and direct sales. Born in Belgium, my beloved husband thought that network marketing was the American dream and tried so many of them. In 1981, I adamantly told him, "If you ever bring an MLM business home, I will divorce you!" I did not want to be a part of the dreaded NFL (no friends left) club. I never endorsed any company or product in my life. I will admit, however, that for about two seconds I did stock my garage with a bunch of lose-weight-quick products that I thought I could share with my family and friends. I did not understand anything about the opportunity at that time and ended up throwing out hundreds of dollars of stale vitamins when no one wanted what I didn't know I even had. My conviction became even stronger. I have to admit, I actually looked down on people who did multilevel marketing. In my uneducated and limited mind-set, I truly believed these people could not get a "real job." I have since come to learn that a job for most is a way to stay just over broke (J.O.B.).

I was thoroughly convinced that I did not need MLMs. I am a successful international motivational speaker and the author of 4 books, one of which was featured on the Oprah Winfrey Show. My co-author, business partner and daughter, Journey, and I have been featured on hundreds of radio and television programs internationally. We are a sought after, unique mother-daughter team that specializes in communication skills for parents and kids. Our work is endorsed by Deepak Chopra, Stephen Covey, Dr. John Gray and Jack Canfield, among others. I was happy and content with my ability to make a difference in the world and loved what I was doing. I was making good money as a professional speaker, but as soon as I stopped speaking — I stopped making money. I was caught in the perpetual loop of frustration. I was always just a little short for the big dreams I had for myself and my two children. Having experienced a bankruptcy in the early years of our marriage, I carried a burden of feeling I never had enough and what if I stopped working, would we ever get ahead?

Fast forward to May 2002. My husband and I were at the wedding of a mutual friend with our dear friend, Dr. John Gray, bestselling author of *Men Are from Mars, Women Are from Venus*. John was telling me about his latest book when the conversation took an odd turn. He began telling me about a nutritional company he discovered that had amazing products that not only helped him to lose unwanted pounds safely and quickly, but he felt a new-found level of energy and felt like he found the fountain of youth. Then, he happily and excitedly said, "It's a network marketing company." Startled, I retorted with, "You're a multi-millionaire and you're selling products out of the trunk of your car? Are you crazy?"

John quickly told me that this particular company was not at all like that. He said that with these stellar products, online tools and resources available — he could build a customer base and a down line as a way to generously repay his family and friends for supporting his work over all these years. My husband jumped on the bandwagon, tried the products and in a relatively short period of time went from a size 44 waist to a 36. His energy shot up, his memory improved and he had more energy in the bedroom. After 28 years of marriage, I was a happy camper!

I quickly gave the products to my kids and everyone I knew. The results were nothing short of phenomenal. Yet, with all the health challenges I had faced over the last eight years, I was still reluctant (and too stubborn) to try the products. Then, one day I was standing in John Gray's kitchen. His beautiful wife Bonnie said, "Andrea, you have struggled with weight, exhaustion and extreme body discomfort and change of life problems for years. Nothing has helped you long enough for you to feel really good. Please just trust me and try this." What she didn't know, is that I felt so horrible most days that I often thought about how it would feel to just leave my body and not have to deal with all this physical deterioration.

With the help and support of friends and family, I finally let down my guard and gave in. I could not believe that I was actually using a network marketing product. Within days, I felt better. Now, after five years of never missing a day of this revolutionary, new food technology, I have released 35 pounds and at 52 years of age, I feel better than I did at 32. I have been truly blessed.

In 2004, I discovered that in this company, I could make money whether I liked it or not. I decided to read about network marketing and opened my mind to residual income. I found that by sharing these miraculous products with my family, friends and colleagues, my yearly income could become my weekly income. What's more, I can do this while laying on a beach in Cancun! Once the residual income bug bit, I was hooked.

In just 2.5 short years, I have created a residual multiple 6-figure income for myself. In this last year, I helped 5 families create the same for themselves. In my quest for knowledge, I became a researcher of products and ingredients and have not found any other product or company that comes close to the one I have found. I have written 3 books on health and wellness for families and created 2 audio CD's for this company. I am proud to say that as of this writing, I have built a very successful down line of approximately 9,000 people.

I never became part of the NFL Club; in fact, my friendship circle has expanded far beyond my wildest dreams. I have team members that I love as much as my family. We work together, we train together and we go on company cruises. We encourage one another and make sure that every new person that joins our "family" gets plugged into our network of training and support. In our company, you are in business for yourself, but not by yourself. The cross team support is heart-warming and changing the MLM industry: no one has "secrets," we all share our successes and wins. The CEOs, presidents, vice presidents and customer service team all act as supporting family members. This company has created 20 millionaires in just 5 short years and the potential is huge for everyone just beginning.

In all my years of travel, working with corporations, associations and organizations, I have never witnessed anything like this nutritional company I was so reluctant to join. But since becoming a product user, I am now a trainer and one of the top 100 earners in the company. If I can do it, anyone can do it. There is nothing as freeing as network marketing once you have found the right product, the company and the best compensation plan in the world. I feel free. I am healthy. And I am a firm believer that network marketing is the way to achieve true wealth in the form of time and financial freedom. I am grateful to this amazing company that I am proud to endorse. I am also grateful to Bonnie and John Gray for their gentle persistence. I truly believe that everything I have done in my life has lead me to this moment, right here and right now.

On behalf of my husband, and my two children, my daughter Journey, age 26 and my son Quest, age 20, this company has helped us get even healthier and has truly set us all free. There is nothing sweeter than watching your own children find the key to health, wealth and wellness at an early age. We are truly blessed and together, we are making a huge difference in all the lives we touch.

Andrea Frank Henkart
California, USA

BITTEN BY THE MLM BUG

In the 1980s, I was a single woman working 60-80 hours a week as an accountant in a hospital; I also had a ceramic business, selling gifts and teaching classes. To start my business I took out a loan using three properties as collateral. For five years business was great; then it began a downward spiral. In 1986 the bank foreclosed on my loan, taking my three properties. I became despondent and actually made plans to have a car accident to end my life so the insurance would provide money for my mother to pay my bills and save my "good name reputation".

A business woman called and invited me to an opportunity meeting. I declined her invitation at first, knowing that I didn't need the opportunity, because I already had my plan. However, I was broke and hungry and she promised to buy me a hamburger when we went, so I agreed to attend with her. That weekend she paid my way to see and hear about the opportunity. After attending the weekend event, I saw a value in their courses and made up my mind that I would get the money to join. This business did not cost hundreds of dollars to start, but thousands. Within sixty days of working the business, I had doubled the money it cost to get started; and I was able to pay the delinquent payments and save my business. I had been bitten by the MLM bug; this was to change my life.

At the annual convention, I met an awesome man who was a leader in that company. A year later we were married, and continued working in multi-level marketing together. After helping many people achieve their goals, we became wealthy and decided to retire and enjoy life on the farm in Tennessee. However, we are people who had always been active and we found we weren't ready to retire. My husband decided he wanted a "real job" and I once again opened another commercial business. Soon after, a former MLM friend called about another opportunity and I was soon home-based again. As before, I enjoyed the success and the satisfaction of assisting others to have a better life. After several years, my dreams shattered as the pay checks from the company stopped and it folded. Despite my bad experience, I began a period of joining every company that looked promising, searching for the golden opportunity. Instead of earning money I was raising the balance on credit cards to the limit and then getting another one. Finally, my husband issued me the ultimatum that "If I did another one of those 'things', he would divorce me." The desire to experience the thrill and excitement I felt when I helped others reach their goals was still burning deep within me. Because of my love for him and a desire to honor his wishes, I declined every offer that presented itself...until a company with a product we really needed came along.

The product worked and the company was a dream come true. This company appeared to have everything good that I had seen in other companies and more. By promising that I would never join another company, if I did not succeed in this one, my husband gave me his approval. Guess what? Now, he is my partner in the business and we are achieving our goals and having fun helping others build their businesses and have their dreams come true.

The tips I would offer other women include:

- Be the kind of person you would love to have in your business.
- Take your eyes off yourself and put them on other people.
- When you see something you deeply desire, go for it with enthusiasm.
- Enthusiasm is the bridge between poverty and prosperity.

- Surround yourself with positive, excited, happy people who love what they are doing.

- Be the best you can be...one breath at a time.

- Never, never settle for less than what you dream to have.

- Never allow anyone to steal your dreams from you.

- And Remember: You can have anything, do anything, be anybody and go anywhere, when you dream BIG DREAMS and work to make those dreams come true.

Charlene Patterson
Tennessee, USA

I AM MY OWN BOSS

I am a retired registered nurse and a mother of five girls between the ages of 8 and 17! My husband is a chiropractor and as a result health has always been a big part of our life and we live a very healthy lifestyle. I did not work outside the home for many years as I was raising our children and yes, raising 5 girls is a full time job! As the children got older I started to get restless and felt like I wanted to add some more opportunities to my family's life. My husband and I have big dreams for our family, and I felt like I wanted to start to earn some dollars so we could fulfill those dreams. I was not interested in going back to shift work because it did not fit our family's lifestyle.

An MLM company came into my life — seemingly by coincidence — assuming there are any coincidences! My health had been suffering as I had been feeling very cloudy, not mentally sharp and I was forgetting more than my fair share of things. This was quite unlike me and it was starting to interfere with my quality of life. My husband and I tried several things within our spectrum of health choices and nothing seemed to be helping. Finally, we sent the intention out that we were looking for something that would help with my health and get me back to my old self.

My husband had a fellow chiropractor tell him of an experience he recently had with some amazing products. He casually mentioned that this was an amazing business opportunity as well and he asked my husband if we might like to try the products. Feeling this was a sign, I read everything I could about the products and the company. We decided it would not hurt to give the products a try but I told my husband's colleague that I did not want anything to do with the business. I did not like MLM and could not see how I could make any money at it as I was not a sales person.

To keep this story short, I experienced amazing results and I felt the best I had in years. I was mentally sharp, I lost 13 pounds and 20 inches and I had people asking me what I was using on my face because it looked very clear. They also asked what shampoo I was using because my hair was unbelievably shiny. My husband also had very similar results.

After getting such great results how could I NOT tell my family and friends about these amazing products. However, I was still nervous of the whole "MLM thing," yet I sucked it up and went back to that chiropractor and told him that I wanted to learn about the business. It was exactly what I was looking for, a passive income stream that allows me to work from home and contribute to the manifestation of my family's dream! Through this company I feel like I am using the best of my nursing knowledge and continuing to work in the health care field, coaching people to better health and leading them through the business if they choose.

What I love about this product and company is that I can work the hours that I want from my own home and I can still keep my family's needs at the top of my priority list. I don't have to ask for time off to support my children at their important events and I don't even have to get dressed if I don't feel like it. I am my own boss, yet I have a huge support system above me at my finger tips any time I need them. I don't ever feel alone. I am now working the business full time and I am excited about my life again and all the possibilities it holds for me and my family!

Shelley Preston
Ontario, Canada

MY LIFE WAS TRANSFORMED THROUGH MULTILEVEL MARKETING

I love and admire my husband Rob, and we have 3 amazing children. I signed into my first network marketing opportunity less then 2 years ago. I was very reluctant to even look at the opportunity and went to a meeting just to get a friend to stop bugging me.

I have to tell you I had a boulder on my shoulder about network marketing companies. But what I learned is that I was afraid of something that I knew nothing about. What I realize now is that if you like people, you will love network marketing. I have found that we are attracting the highest quality people- the kind of people I want to spend my time with. I actually miss them when I am not around them.

In 2 years we have built an organization with over 80,000 people and it grows by 2000 people a week. This opportunity has created a multi-million dollar income stream for my family, which has allowed us to truly live our dreams. As I have never done network marketing before I wanted to share what we did that gave us so much success so quickly. I really want you to understand that if I can do this so can you.

There are 3 things that I would credit most to my success in this industry. What I did was look at my strengths and apply them into the network marketing model.

1. I built relationships.

2. I am selective about sponsoring.

3. I focused on developing leaders.

Build Relationships

Network marketing opportunities are truly a blessing for women. Where else can you have no glass ceiling and get paid for talking? I built my business without a website and without any tools. I built a high touch- low tech business. I built relationships by setting up everyone that I sponsored to win. I gave them all that they would need to start their business, taught them what to do immediately, and then told them to call me everyday. When your focus is on helping others succeed it's only a matter of time before you will succeed.

The added advantage of this business is that you will meet some of the best quality people. Imagine vacationing around the world with your families together as you build this business of relationships. There is simply no greater joy.

Be Selective

I don't invite everyone that I meet into my business. I know that anyone that I sponsor I go to work for. Therefore, I am choosy. I look for people with a good work ethic and the right attitude. I don't want people who will pull me down. In your regular jobs you don't usually get to select who works next to you. In a network marketing opportunity you get to pick who you work with. So I have always known it is important to surround yourself with like minded, positive people of integrity.

Develop Leaders

My goal has been to develop a HUGE team of leaders. This is achieved first and foremost through developing friendships. Giving others the skills, confidence, and encouragement is what helps them succeed. I love to stand beside my friends to watch them blossom into their full light as their friend, mentor, and business partner.

While I did these 3 things I also had a personal attitude that I wanted to share with you. I have long believed that true happiness comes from serving others. I serve others by helping them get to their goals. My dream has been to touch millions of people and I know that I can't do this alone. This is only done if I personally touch hundreds and they personally touch hundreds.

So whatever your strengths are, use them. Whatever you believe you are missing, sponsor that type of person into your business. And above all, work the business as a team.

Onyx Coale
Florida, USA

THE MIRACLE OF NETWORK MARKETING AND ME

Just a year ago, I was a busy single mother of three young teenagers and a psychotherapist who filled any spare time with exercise, coffee with friends, helping clients, volunteer work, and driving my kids; yet, I knew there was something missing day-to-day. I WAS BORED – and didn't know it! The day my love, Alan, came home and told me he was not only starting with some new nutritional products, but he was attending a TRAINING that weekend about the network marketing opportunity, I felt very threatened by this unknown "thing." To use the word skeptical would be an understatement! As a well-educated nurse and counseling therapist, not to mention daughter of two MBA parents, I was certain that network marketing was not a real business model.

One month later, after Alan looked and felt fabulous, I was intrigued enough to look into it. I reluctantly tried the products and then a new network marketer was born! Literally almost every person I knew wanted to use what I was using, do what I was doing. I enthusiastically shared my story. That's it. By February, I had a call from the company head office saying that I had won a contest for an all expenses paid trip to the annual convention and a shopping spree with the co-founders! The health-care profession NEVER rewarded effort and work like this!

It is now less than one year ago that I began this adventure and adventure it has been. I have experienced phenomenal personal growth; I have learned that I am creative, an entrepreneur and a leader. I inspire others to be the best they can be! I inspire myself and my children and I LOVE what I do everyday. I get to help people and be rewarded. I get to learn from mentors who motivate, teach, and encourage me – all from the comfort of my home.

To all women, I strongly suggest to reach beyond what you think is possible and be open to all that this wonderful life has to offer – especially the opportunities that network marketing brings. There is nothing else like it. It is THE best business model for women. It allows you to truly have it all: family, fulfillment, fortune, freedom.

Camille Lawson
Ontario, Canada

BUILDING A HEALTHY, WEALTHY AND BRIGHT FUTURE

I let someone change my life. I had no idea it would be through a nutritional product and a multilevel marketing company. But I am so excited that it was!

I was sick for 10 years. How did that happen? I didn't plan for that! How did I find myself in this position? When I had children I started putting myself last. Over the years things got out of control and I allowed myself to become shortchanged in life. I was following my mom's example of how she raised me and as a result I was getting all my mom's illnesses and some of my own as well. I was scared. I was angry. I had dark days on the couch. I was unable to climb a flight of stairs. I was so exhausted by mid afternoon that I could hardly get supper ready for my family. I was sick and tired of being sick and tired. I was gaining more and more weight and when I'd diet I would lose 1 pound only to gain back 2-3.

When a friend told me about a nutritional product I didn't realize the impact it would have on my life. He also told me it was sold through an MLM company, which I didn't understand at all. But I did understand this: my medical bills were $1000.00 a month more than insurance would cover. I needed my health back and I needed to increase my income so I said, "Yes, I want that stuff NOW." That was a no-brainer. I'm blonde but I figured that one out!

Within days of taking this product I noticed better health. Because my health improved, my outlook and my self-confidence improved. As a result I decided to market this product and tackle the challenge of building my own MLM business. I've lost a total of 60 pounds and I'm continuing to lose weight. While I am expanding my MLM business I'm shrinking myself! It's so great! And it's so great to see lives changed through improved health and increased wealth as I help women who suffered as I used to! This product and MLM company are the tools I needed to start taking care of myself again both physically and financially. They are the tools I, and many other women, need to balance our lives and to put ourselves first. I work this business part time and in those few hours I dedicate to it each day, I have full confidence that my future is bright, healthy and wealthy, and so are the lives of many women who choose to work an MLM business.

Cindy Loewen
St. Lazare, Quebec

MLM MOM

Network marketing, as an industry, is a phenomenal opportunity. When I was trading time for money, it was a finite process. Women are masters of multitasking in general. We are experts at juggling family, work, school or community involvement, caring for aging parents, etc.

Network marketing allows you to multitask to the infinite extent of the word. It turns everyday activities into relationship building opportunities that create an infinite world of possibilities. That doesn't mean that there is no focus. This business has helped me focus my energies. I have developed my talents in connecting and building relationships, which is what speaks most to me, while at the same time building a profitable business. It has encouraged me to stretch myself beyond my comfort zone, beyond what I was capable, and sometimes throws me into a new level of my comfort, only to push me beyond again. I have learned new ideas, paradigms and ways of communicating, which are always assisting me professionally and personally. I have shared these with my husband and children, and know they are having a positive impact. I involve my family in my business in a very real way. They know many of the people I work with because many are long-time friends. They've also met wonderful people who have now become new, dear friends because of the focus on team-building.

I have never seen any other opportunity in the work force that emphasizes dream building and reaching for the stars, as much as network marketing. Finding the right company that resonates with who you are and what your vision is for your future, is key. I have been able to align my personal and professional philosophies in an industry that provides me with the flexibility to work around my family's needs and schedules. At the same time, I am pursuing my own personal and professional interests, while making a substantial part-time — transforming to full-time — income.

I am grateful for the right opportunity at the right time in my life. Network marketing is not to be overlooked.

Joanne Mulhall
British Columbia, Canada

WE ARE THE LUCKIEST WOMEN IN THE WORLD

My journey into the industry of network marketing, like many women, was to fulfill a need. In my case, it was a need for more income, more time to be present for my seven children and a need to have it all. I wanted income to not only float our boat, but to flourish, to have choices I knew were our birthright: college tuitions, car insurances, and more than anything I wanted to have precious time. I wanted time to enjoy my children, who were quickly growing up.

I also felt extremely lucky I had a great husband, Tom, who is the best. He is someone that just put his head down and went to work, often 15 hour days, 7 days a week. He never complained and he was such a great father. I knew if my children were to enjoy their dad, there was no way he could physically keep going. Luckily God gave me seven healthy, happy, fun children, four who were all in college at the same time, talk about financial responsibility. I also had a great big way, one that spells Go-Go-Go, I ran a daycare from my home and I also worked weekend nights, 30 hours a weekend.

I was introduced to my first network marketing company by my father in 1983. As I began to understand the power of residual income and leverage, I saw what was possible and went to work. I was very lucky because as a family, Tom and our children, I had a great support system. Our children also knew how important our success meant to their lives. I was also blessed because I had a wonderful coach and mentor, my dad, whom I not only respected, but felt confident that he would teach me everything I needed to learn.

After years of persistence, my prayers were answered in a very big way. I am now one of the top income earners in my present company. Network marketing is all about people. Many of the people are women, moms, who truly want it all and become unstoppable. I knew what my strengths were, and I also understood the importance of teamwork. The power of teams of people, from all walks of life, with a common mission. I love network marketing because it allows us to shine, our God given talents, each of us working together toward a common goal.

I also feel extremely lucky, because I finally learned to become patient, and allow God to really guide me to the right people. Believe me there were days I wanted to go 100 miles ahead and fast, but like all good things, you have to trust the process. You have to believe in yourself and your team! Celebrate your success; celebrating is a true form of gratitude. There isn't a second of each day that I don't thank God for all of our success, and the growing success of our amazing teams.

What network marketing does is it allows for women to have it all. Great relationships are priceless, to become better people, friends, moms, wives. The personal development just moves you forward from the inside out. Do I feel blessed? Absolutely, I went from working 80 hours a week, long hard hours, with very little financial stability, to real peace of mind, priceless. I have now replaced both my income along with my husband's income and now I get to spend each day working with my husband from the comfort of my home. Now talk about dreams coming true! Absolutely, no matter what you dream to be, to have, network marketing is your vehicle. As a little girl, I learned to develop an over the top attitude. Attitude is more important then anything in life! Do what you love, learn your skills, practice and treat your network marketing business with the right attitude. Your dreams will all come true! When you feel like the luckiest person in the world and ask yourself daily, "What is great about this?" God will share his answers, don't forget to listen, just do it with praise and passion. The most beautiful piece about life is people helping connecting with other people, making a difference. I am so grateful for all the talented, beautiful, passionate women that I get to team up with. I get to grow with them and cherish their success. Have it all, yes we are the luckiest women in the world!

Thank you everyone!

Kathy Smith
Pennsylvania, USA

HELPING OTHERS BY BEING TRUE TO OURSELVES

Let me introduce myself. My name is Dianne. At the age of nine, I taught my three-year-old sister, Angel how to read. Our parents were great in sales but steered us into stable but stressful professional positions,

positions with strict hours, little opportunity for advancement, few financial incentives and a forest of paperwork resulting from governmental rules and regulations. In order to meet the demands of our careers in education and social work, we had been putting our unfulfilled dreams and talents under a bushel. Nevertheless, we were able to retire early from these jobs and to collect very limited pensions that paid our bills but not much more.

Why did we leave the comfort of retirement?

My sister and I believe we are expected to freely share our God-given talents with everyone we meet. No longer encumbered by the restrictions of our former careers, we are able to express our true selves (Angel the musician and Di the herbalist) and realize our dreams by seizing the day and letting our light shine. We can balance work, play and dreams.

How and why did we become involved in network marketing?

Although Angel and I had dabbled in a few other networking companies in the past, it was my chiropractor who introduced us to our present company. We were so excited by this company's essential oils, so in love with their fragrances and their benefits and so thrilled by the limitless financial opportunity and freedom of MLM that we decided to use essential oils as the basis of our MLM business to which we brought our love of people and respect for the environment. To us, multilevel, network or relationship marketing is a direct way to help people unleash, improve and share their talents with others and to have fun in the process. In MLM, founded on trust and cooperation, personal efforts to aid others profit both giver and receiver. An anonymous quote on a business card phrased it this way: "The fragrance of the rose lingers on the hand of the giver."

What tips do we have for women?

Follow your heart. Dream big. Never fear, only believe. Let your light shine.

Dianne Tzouras & *Angel Brock*
Pennsylvania, USA   Michigan, USA

MLM Woman Conclusion

What if this life you truly dream of is wrapped up in a package called multilevel marketing? What if you can truly have more time with your family, nurture yourself and do everything you dream, and the vehicle that ferries you to that destination is free enterprise? This book is full of women who are living their dreams and you can be one of us. This isn't about the destination; it is about the journey.

There will be times of challenge. There will be moments you question your decision. There may even be times when others are not as supportive of your dreams. The truth is that it does get better and better; the longer you persist the more you learn and the more you learn the greater you become. That is where abundance and ease partner in your life.

The biggest secret of MLM is to be grateful for everything you already have. Be grateful for every challenge because each one is simply a lesson. Be grateful for every victory because if you can do something once, you can surely do it again. Gratitude will make the journey even richer.

To be an MLM woman is simply a decision. Know in your heart that you are truly making a difference. Unlike a job where you trade time for dollars, you have the ability to get paid what you are truly worth. You have the power to liberate people everywhere and impact lives.

Imagine a nation where people could work from home. It would cut down on emissions from cars; people would have more time with their families. People everywhere could be present in their lives. You have the power to initiate this kind of change. You have the power to make dreams come true.

We encourage you to become an ambassador of multilevel marketing. Be proud of your industry. Read books, like this one and others, to educate you on the power of MLM. Attend seminars and events. Be a sponge for knowledge. Just imagine the person you are already becoming.

Within you lies a great MLM woman. Go forward and share your knowledge with others. We truly look forward to seeing you at the top.

Susan and Suzan

Glossary

Associate / Affiliate: To be associated with a network marketing company. An individual who has enrolled as a member and is most often able to purchase products at a reduced price. Often referred to as a distributor, this individual is also in a position to build an organization and generate income.

Collecting a decision: To ask for the sale.

Down line: All associates located below you in your team. This would include associates that you have personally sponsored as well as those sponsored by other associates below you.

Prospect: An individual you desire to introduce to your company's products, service and/or business opportunity.

Prospecting: The act of connecting with an individual or group with the intention to share information about your products, service and opportunity.

Sponsor: An associate who has enrolled one or more associates. To sponsor means to take responsibility for. A sponsor is responsible for training, guiding and supporting a new associate.

Up line: All associates located above you in a team. This would include your personal sponsor.

Volume: Every company assigns an amount of volume to a sale. Generally there is a sales volume created from the purchase of products or services.

TERMS FROM SUSAN & SUZAN

Abundance: To be prosperous. To have wealth in all areas of your life. The ability to produce in all areas of your life.

Anchor: To attach or secure an intention to something you can see, feel, touch or hear.

Auditory Filter: An inner filter that presides as judge over both sender and message so that when we actually receive the message, it has been transformed to fit our expectations and conform to what we want to hear.

Balance: To be committed and present in all areas of your life.

Clearing: To create physical space by letting go of unnecessary possessions. To create emotional space by releasing emotional baggage. To create space by setting aside time or choosing to give up an activity or commitment.

Self Mastery: Self awareness. The ability to manage your thoughts, emotions and actions. It is to take responsibility for your choices.

Susan Sly is a successful entrepreneur, author, speaker, master trainer, certified nutritional consultant, certified trainer and coach with over 15 years of experience in health and wellness. She has also generated over $20 million in sales in the industry of network marketing.

Susan has been a professor of nutrition at St. Lawrence College in Kingston and a guest lecturer for The Queen's University School of Business, Queen's University School of Environmental Science and George Brown College in Toronto. She was also the top producing North American sales manager for Bally Total Fitness.

Susan has competed for Team Canada six times both in Track and Field and Duathlon. She has competed in two World Championships. She placed in the top 10 in the pro division of the Ironman in Malaysia in 2001. In 2007 Susan completed the Boston Marathon.

Susan is an in-demand motivational speaker and has shared the stage with Mark Victor Hansen, Jim Rohn and more. Susan is a success coach and speaker who has helped co-create numerous six figure earners.

From the years of 1997 to present, Susan has been featured on television, radio, print media and has speaking engagements booked into next year.

Susan has three children, ages 2, 5 and 11 years and is the devoted wife to her life partner Chris Arkeveld. Susan and Chris dedicate time to giving back and are currently involved in a fund raising project with World Vision to support a trauma center for girls rescued from brothels and sexual trauma in Cambodia. Susan and Chris also sponsor 20 children through World Vision.

Susan is the author of the best selling book *The Have It All Woman*. She is the co-founder of the Have It All Woman's Weekend where women undergo three days of life changing personal empowerment. Susan is the president and CEO of Step Into Your Power Productions, a company dedicated to teaching individuals how to create more abundance in their lives. Her website is www.stepintoyourpower.com.

. . . .

 **Suzan Hart** was born in Port of Spain, Trinidad. When Suzan was five years old, her family immigrated to Canada were they settled in a small college town in eastern Quebec. The youngest daughter of Lorna Gordon, Suzan believes she gets her drive and "never give up attitude" from watching her mother triumph, creating diamonds from coal.

Suzan Hart is a master trainer, speaker and coach. She travels all over North America sharing the message of personal empowerment for anyone looking to take charge of his or her life. Suzan is committed to assisting her clients in creating abundance and ease by enhancing their leadership.

A successful entrepreneur, Suzan is a multiple six figure earner in the industry of network marketing. Building a reputation as an industry trainer, Suzan is a lead trainer and success coach at Step Into Your Power. Suzan, in partnership with Susan Sly, is the co-founder of the Have It All Woman's Weekend, a three-day, life-changing workshop.

With more than 10 years experience, Suzan is a highly effective family, individual and group counselor. Trained in crisis and mediation, she has worked extensively in the area of child welfare and women's services. Suzan has managed a women's shelter, a cross cultural counseling service, as well as one of the largest drop-in centers in the down town core of the city of Toronto.

The founder and president of Hart Consulting, Suzan has a brilliant capacity to engage the individual, groups, management and organizational structures. As a result, she has a reputation for causing leadership and developing healthy, productive and cohesive teams.

With an extensive background in group dynamics, Suzan has an enhanced ability to coach in the areas of conflict, change, management, communication, cultural competency and leadership.

An accomplished athlete, Suzan has experienced success in the areas of track, basketball and competitive body building. As an entrepreneur Suzan believes that true wealth begins with a healthy mind, body and soul. Together with Susan Sly, Suzan has co-founded MBC, a telecourse designed to have one's physical and emotional health as the foundation for abundance and wealth.

Suzan Hart's mission is to create an environment where all individuals feel inspired, valued and honored for their contribution, such that they take bold action and create abundance with ease.